MW01193945

Palmito Ranch

Palmito Ranch

FROM CIVIL WAR BATTLEFIELD TO NATIONAL HISTORIC LANDMARK

Jody Edward Ginn and
William Alexander McWhorter

Foreword by
Richard B. McCaslin

TEXAS A&M UNIVERSITY PRESS
COLLEGE STATION

Copyright © 2018 by Texas Historical Commission
All rights reserved
First edition

This paper meets the requirements of ANSI/NISO Z39.48–1992
(Permanence of Paper).
Binding materials have been chosen for durability.
Manufactured in China through Four Color Print Group.

Library of Congress Cataloging-in-Publication Data

Names: Ginn, Jody Edward, 1969– author. | McWhorter, William Alexander,
1975–author. | McCaslin, Richard B., writer of foreword.
Title: Palmito Ranch : from Civil War battlefield to national historic
  landmark / Jody Edward Ginn and William Alexander McWhorter.
Description: First edition. | College Station : Texas A&M University Press,
  [2018] | Includes bibliographical references and index.
Identifiers: LCCN 2017058031| ISBN 9781623496364 (book/flexbound : alk.
  paper) | ISBN 9781623496371 (e-book)
Subjects: LCSH: Palmito Ranch, Battle of, Tex., 1865. | Ford, John Salmon. |
  Battlefield monuments—Texas—Palmito Ranch. | Palmito Ranch
  (Tex.)—History, Military. | Historic sites—Conservation and
  restoration—Cameron County—Texas. | United States—History—Civil War,
  1861-1865—Historiography. | United States—History—Civil War,
  1861-1865—Influence. | Heritage tourism—Texas. | Texas Historical
  Commission.
Classification: LCC E477.8 .G56 2018 | DDC 355.009764/495—dc23 LC record
available at https://lccn.loc.gov/2017058031

Contents

Foreword

Texans, native and adopted, love their history. As well they should, because the story of the Lone Star State is an essential component in defining the modern United States. But for so many Texans, like so many of their fellow Americans, the details of the past fade into obscurity, and history often gives way to myth. Texas schoolchildren for decades could recite the names of the three battles in which Texas Confederates repelled Federal invasions of their state during the Civil War: Galveston, Sabine Pass, and Palmito Ranch. Today Sabine Pass and Palmito Ranch are unknown to an increasing number of Texans, especially as the location of Civil War battles, and Galveston is recalled most often as a leading vacation spot. An observant traveler to Galveston, however, will find markers recalling the battle on New Year's Day in 1863 for control of that old port city, and it would be very difficult for any visitor to the state historical park at Sabine Pass to overlook the dramatic statue of Lt. Richard W. Dowling, whose gunners in September 1863 blocked the second attempt by a Union landing force to establish a beachhead in Texas there. Palmito Ranch, located in a relatively isolated corner of southern Texas, has not benefited from the same level of attention as the other two members of the Texas trio of Civil War triumphs. The Texas Historical Commission, through the laudable efforts of William A. McWhorter and Jody E. Ginn, along with a tremendous host of staff and allies, has worked hard to recall to public memory the history of the two battles at Palmito Ranch, the first in September 1864 and the second in May 1865, which earned it the enduring title "Last Land Battle of the Civil War." This book is yet another important step in that effort.

The obscurity of the battles at Palmito Ranch is perhaps odd because both were won by John S. "Rip" Ford, whom a prominent Federal officer,

Maj. Gen. Lew Wallace, described to his boss, Gen. Ulysses S. Grant, as the "most influential Confederate soldier in Texas." Ford began the Civil War with an impressive military résumé, having fought as a US Army officer against Mexicans, as a Texas Ranger commander against Comanches and Mexicans, and even as a Mexican brigadier general in one of the many revolutions along the Rio Grande. Ford swiftly accomplished his initial assignment as a Confederate colonel of removing the Federal garrisons from their posts along the Rio Grande in 1861, but he lost his Confederate commission when his border loyalties led him to disregard orders from Richmond. His popularity in Texas prompted his appointment to supervise the draft in the Lone Star State, a task he accomplished as gently as possible. When Union forces occupied the Gulf Coast of Texas from Corpus Christi south in the fall of 1863, Ford was asked to raise the Rio Grande Expeditionary Force to counter them, with a commission as a brigadier general of Texas state troops. He subsequently won two battles at Palmito Ranch in defense of Brownsville, which he had reoccupied in the late summer of 1864 as the Federals in the area withdrew to Brazos Island at the mouth of the Rio Grande. Ginn narrates those clashes well in this book.

The disappearance of Palmito Ranch from many historical narratives of the Civil War is equally puzzling because of the importance of the Rio Grande region, and indeed all the Texas border with Mexico, to the administration of Abraham Lincoln. Eliminating the Confederate armies and crushing Southerners' willingness to continue their resistance became crucial to the Union war effort, and this was made much more difficult by the trade through Texas and across the Rio Grande. Ford played a key role in developing this in early 1862, when he arranged for ships owned by Texas Confederates and others to fly the Mexican flag as they slipped through the Federal blockade downriver from Brownsville and its sister city, Matamoros. When he took Brownsville in 1864, Ford quickly arranged for a resumption of the commerce that had briefly been interrupted by the Union incursion. Records of the exact value of that activity are hard to find, but Wallace, who visited in March 1865, reported there were more ships at the mouth of the Rio Grande than there were in Baltimore harbor. And many years after the war, Texas rancher Richard King allegedly deposited money each month in Ford's bank account in gratitude for his destitute colleague's efforts on behalf of wartime trade.

Ford did not just promote commerce along the Rio Grande; he also cultivated diplomatic alliances. He pragmatically courted the support of the

French military forces, who had occupied much of Mexico, in 1864 even as the Union officers on Brazos Island welcomed the overtures of Ford's old nemesis, Juan N. Cortina, who had taken Matamoros. The Federals and their Mexican allies lost to Ford at Palmito Ranch in September 1864, after which the French took Matamoros. Ford developed a good working relationship with Gen. Tomas Mejía, Mexican commander of the Matamoros garrison, and French gunners fought alongside the Texans in Ford's final victory in May 1865. All of this was troubling to Lincoln, who focused on isolating the Confederacy diplomatically from potential European allies, including the ambitious emperor Louis Napoleon of France. When Ford slipped across the Rio Grande in the early summer of 1865 and accepted a commission as a brigadier general from Mejía in Matamoros, tens of thousands of Union troops landed in Texas and moved swiftly to secure the Texas border and prevent any last-ditch efforts to forge an alliance between the dying Confederacy and the French occupation forces in Mexico.

Palmito Ranch was thus of great importance not only to Texans, who embraced Ford's victory in the last land battle of the Civil War as one of three triumphs they celebrated as part of the "Lost Cause" mythology of Lone Star invincibility, but also to their Federal adversaries in the war. But the railroads bypassed Brownsville, which had to wait until the twentieth century for substantial development. As Ginn observes in his narrative, that growth did not really affect the site of the two Civil War battles. There were markers placed for the centennial celebration of Texas independence, but few visitors came. The first substantial interest shown by government agencies ironically resulted from a concern for the preservation of the unique flora and fauna in the remote region. Fortunately, these same organizations proved to be good allies in battlefield preservation for the Texas Historical Commission, as did local agencies such as the Cameron County Historical Commission. With their help, the mission of the state historical site can be expanded even further, perhaps exploring the roles played by Tejanos (Refugio Benavides led a company under Ford), African Americans (the 62nd Infantry, US Colored Troops, fought in May 1865 at Palmito Ranch), Texas Unionists (a detachment from the 2nd Texas Cavalry, USA, also served at Palmito Ranch in May 1865), and even women (Ford's many concerns during the September 1864 battle included his young wife, Addie, who insisted on staying with him as he directed the defense of Brownsville). In sum, as one investigates the history of what happened at Palmito Ranch, an increasingly complex story emerges to engage even more Texans.

When I first visited the Palmito Ranch Battlefield in 2009, I completely missed the turn for the site. Today, much less than a decade later, there are not only several markers but also a radio transmitter and a viewing platform. Crowds have gathered at Palmito Ranch for a series of Park Days, and the location has become part of a growing list of sites managed by a revitalized Texas Historical Commission. Much of the credit for that has to go to McWhorter, who would probably refuse such a well-deserved compliment since he fully understands the importance of teamwork in this accomplishment. But teams need leaders, and he has become a leading figure in making sure that Texans who are truly interested in their history step away from the vagaries of myth and embrace the even better true stories. He enlisted Ginn to record a proper narrative of not only the battles in both 1864 and 1865 but also the struggles to rescue Palmito Ranch from obscurity and restore it to its proper place in Texas history. As a state historical site, as well as a wildlife refuge, Palmito Ranch will help bring historical tourists to South Texas, where they can learn on-site about the last land battle of the Civil War. This will ultimately enhance Texans' understanding of their state's role in the Civil War, which was made more complicated by being a focal point for trade and diplomacy. But then, that is what makes Texas history so much fun and why so many of us love it.

—Richard B. McCaslin
University of North Texas

Acknowledgments

The authors' completion of this book represents more than eight years of research and several trips to Palmito Ranch Battlefield National Historic Landmark, and we thank several people who helped us turn an idea into a book. We thank Richard B. "Rick" McCaslin for his generous contribution of frank, thoughtful, and astute advice throughout this project. Rick's sustained encouragement helped see this project to fruition. We are also honored to include his insightful foreword extolling the virtues of preserving and promulgating the history of the Palmito Ranch Battlefield.

The authors thank John L. Nau III, chairman of the Texas Historical Commission (THC), for his leadership, support, and encouragement during nearly a decade of projects at Palmito Ranch Battlefield. Thanks also go to John Crain and Tom Alexander, commissioners; Mark Wolfe, executive director; Bratten Thomason, former director of the History Program Division; and Bob Brinkman, Marker Program coordinator for their support of the Military Sites Program's efforts to preserve the history of the battlefield, including this book. We also thank former THC chief historian Dan Utley, who, during the twilight of his career at the agency, provided leadership and served as a source of valuable institutional knowledge as the agency undertook new projects at the battlefield in 2007. Furthermore, Utley provided valuable feedback during the editing of this manuscript. We thank Barbara Putrino, former senior projects coordinator of the THC; Chris Florence, division director; and their colleagues in the Public Information and Education Division for editing drafts of this manuscript.

Researchers who travel to the Nita Stewart Haley Memorial Library and J. Evetts Haley History Center in Midland are the beneficiaries of wonderful archivists. Thanks to J. Evetts Haley Jr., the authors completed their research into the John S. Ford Papers, part of the Texas Confederate Museum Collection. The authors gratefully acknowledge archivist Jim Bradshaw for his assistance with detailed indexes he created for the Ford Papers during our two research trips in 2009 and 2010. We are also grateful to archivist Cathy Smith, who during the authors' final research trip in 2014 provided professional service in meeting our many requests for primary documents.

In no specific order, we thank a number of other archivists and talented individuals who aided our research: Tonia Wood, reference archivist at the Texas State Library and Archives Commission, and her colleagues for their expedient retrieval of primary documents that facilitated our research; Millie Hernandez, exhibits coordinator for the Special Collections and Archives in Brownsville at the University of Texas Rio Grande Valley, who provided access to their archives and the only known glossy black-and-white photographs of the 1964 Tourist Information Marker at the battlefield; Janette Garcia, head of Special Collections at the University of Texas–Pan American (now the University of Texas Rio Grande Valley) Library in Edinburg, for providing access to microfilm of the *Brownsville Herald*; and Anne Cook, photo librarian at the Texas Department of Transportation.

Unquestionably, this book would not have been possible without the generosity of the following donors who made projects at or about the battlefield possible: the Society of the Order of the Southern Cross, the National Park Service, the US Fish and Wildlife Service, the Texas Historical Foundation, and especially Fred Morse, who provided a grant that made this book a reality. We thank you all, as well as Sunny Howard and the development offices of the Friends of the Texas Historical Commission— Toni Turner, Lisa Avery, Rebecca Borchers, and Anjali Zutshi—for their invaluable assistance in raising the grants that have helped save Palmito Ranch Battlefield.

William McWhorter thanks his parents. During childhood his father, Ted, instilled in him a solid work ethic that he has tapped whenever a large project has presented itself. His mother, Anne, gave him the patience he has needed throughout life, especially during this project, when so many obstacles had to be surmounted. Last but certainly not least, he thanks his wife, Amy, and daughter, Maya, for their support, love, and consideration during the writing of this book. Amy and Maya are his world; he loves them with his entire heart and dedicates his portion of this book to them.

Jody Edward Ginn thanks his wife, Lesli; his son, Spencer; and his daughter, Katherine, for their patience and support of his work in a field that often requires extended travel and for graciously tolerating his passion for history even when they cannot necessarily relate to the subject at hand.

Finally, the authors thank the partners in preservation that have combined in varying ways to make possible the projects detailed in this book and helped save Palmito Ranch Battlefield. In no specific order, the US Fish and Wildlife Service's South Texas Refuge Complex, specifically the Lower Rio Grande National Wildlife Refuge and Manager Bryan Winton, have exhibited years of continued enthusiastic interest and financial support of projects related to the THC's effort since 2007 to increase the interpretation and preservation of the battlefield. The terrific working partnership with the Palo Alto Battlefield National Historical Park can be attributed in no small part to the unofficial "good-neighbor policy" practiced by the National Park Service. The THC owes a great deal of gratitude to superintendents Mary Kralovek and Mark Spier, as well as Historian Douglas Murphy and Chief of Resource Management Rolando Garza for their years of support of projects associated with Palmito Ranch Battlefield.

The Civil War Sesquicentennial Committee of the Cameron County Historical Commission from the first Park Day in 2008 through the site's sesquicentennial in May 2015 has been a driving force in preserving the history of, and promoting appreciation for, the battle. It has been an honor for the authors to work with Craig Stone, Wilson Bourgeois, and their colleagues. The Brownsville Historical Association has also been a wonderful resource, and their participation in mustering local support has been of great assistance. Russell Skowronek, Roseann Bacha-Garza, and their colleagues at the Rio Grande Valley Civil War Trail have been supportive in driving heritage tourism to the battlefield. Last, we thank the Civil War Trust for its support of the THC's ongoing efforts at Palmito Ranch Battlefield—by providing hallowed ground to survey, resources for Park Day activities for the past nine years, and a cover article in their popular national magazine edition of *Hallowed Ground*. Thank you all.

Palmito Ranch

Introduction

The Little-Known History of the
Battle of Palmito Ranch

In his account of the Battle of Palmito Ranch, "The Last Battle—The Last Charge, and the Last Gun Fired in the War," Confederate cavalryman Capt. Wiley H. D. Carrington of Austin, Texas, recalled hearing the last shots of the Civil War. He reported that as evening fell on May 13, 1865, a shell from either Brazos Island or a nearby Union warship exploded between the two armies. Throughout the eleven states that constituted the Confederate States of America, much was destroyed, and the future was uncertain. As the sound of gunfire died away deep in South Texas, Americans were left with a country forever changed. Many Texans clung to their last victory as evidence that the South had been defeated but Texas had not.[1]

The Civil War was a major turning point in the history of Texas and the United States. The war deeply divided citizens of the Lone Star State. The battles were legendary, and the aftermath of the war deeply scarred the young nation and Texas. The end of the war, the end of slavery, and the beginning of Reconstruction marked a new era for the United States, one in which many Texans struggled to find a new identity.[2]

Seeking to distance themselves from the stigma of the South's "Lost Cause" and the "peculiar institution" of slavery with which it was inextricably linked, Texans during the late nineteenth and early twentieth centuries largely shrugged off their Southern agricultural identity in favor of a western one that idealized notions of rugged individualism and individual liberty. Despite the inconvenient fact that most Texans continued to share more in common with their fellow Southern farmers than with western frontiersmen, Texan politicians and writers of history actively promulgated such myths for generations to come. When they did address Texas' role in the Civil War, it was to emphasize military prowess or the federal over-reach of Radical Republicans later during Reconstruction. This approach informed not only many published works but also the interpretation—or lack thereof—of many historic sites within the Lone Star State.[3]

While the state does not possess monumental Civil War battlefields such as Gettysburg or Antietam, it does have a wealth of military and home-front sites that are important in telling a complete history of the war that divided America. Some are visible, having been restored and interpreted, but others are forgotten, are endangered, or have since been demolished. Regardless of condition, many historic sites are commemorated through museums, monuments, and landmarks that tell their stories. One of the most historically significant Civil War military sites in Texas—both region-ally and nationally—is the Palmito Ranch Battlefield National Historic Landmark. Located twelve miles east of Brownsville on Texas Highway 4, the site lies within a barren stretch of coastal plain near Texas' Rio Grande border with Mexico. It is approximately midway between Brazos Island on the Gulf Coast, a Union army post during the war, and Fort Brown, the antebellum military post held by the Confederates in Brownsville. Despite decades of development in Cameron County and more than 150 years after the battles fought there, remarkably, the battlefield retains substantial his-toric integrity.

The Battle of Palmito Ranch, often referred to as the Battle of Palmito Hill, occurred on May 12 and 13, 1865, when the Civil War was essentially over. Gen. Robert E. Lee, commander of the Confederate Army of North-ern Virginia, had surrendered his forces more than a month earlier at Appomattox Court House. By May 12, 1865, other Confederate troops had capitulated, Confederate president Jefferson Davis had been captured, and the South was reeling from more than four years of war with the North.[4]

For several generations, many historians virtually ignored Texas and most of the Confederate Trans-Mississippi Department when recounting the causes, battles, and aftermath of the American Civil War. In particu-lar, the last land battle of the Civil War was discounted as irrelevant to the conflict overall and, therefore, left out almost altogether from the larger narrative, notwithstanding John S. "Rip" Ford's account in his memoir, published in 1963. However, the last two decades have seen a surge in schol-arly and popular interest in how the Civil War affected Texas and how Texas contributed to and influenced the conflict. The battlefield is significant as the site of the last battle, but there was also another battle fought there. These two battles, along with the battlefield's proximity to the border with Mexico and the cross-border cotton trade during the war (essential to the Confederacy war effort), shed light on the historical importance and national significance of the last battle.[5]

Beginning with Noah Andre Trudeau's *Out of the Storm*, published in 1994, Palmito Ranch has received long-overdue attention. Trudeau provided an overview of the May 1865 battle and the events that led to it in an interesting, yet highly condensed narrative.[6] Trudeau's work, although concise, appears to have served as a catalyst for further study of the battle; by the turn of the twenty-first century, two book-length publications appeared that specifically chronicled the Battle of Palmito Ranch: Philip Thomas Tucker's *The Final Fury: Palmito Ranch, the Last Battle of the Civil War* (2001) and Jeffrey William Hunt's *The Last Battle of the Civil War: Palmetto Hill* (2002).

The Final Fury is an accessible and evocative account—long on speculation regarding the various participants' motives and mind-sets but short on documentation and evidence. The historical record does not support several of Tucker's factual assertions, including his claims regarding the brutal treatment of Union soldiers taken prisoner by Confederate Texans at the earlier Battle of Las Rucias Ranch in June 1864.[7] Tucker's casualty estimates are not supported by the available primary-source documents, and they lack corroborating evidence for his deviations.[8] However, Tucker produced the first book-length publication regarding the last battle of the Civil War at Palmito Ranch, and his contribution is noted.

The Last Battle of the Civil War is a more scholarly account of the engagement. Hunt relies on the substantial volumes of evidence available in the historical record, carefully comparing and contrasting the various accounts and reports to determine their credibility. As a result, Hunt provides a balanced, nuanced, and thoroughly documented interpretation of the relevant events preceding, during, and immediately after the battle. Hunt clears the air regarding all outstanding major issues of fact surrounding the battle, including troop numbers, casualties, Union prisoners taken, and movements throughout the encounter.[9]

Hunt concludes that the Confederate losses were far lighter than often reported. The author estimates, based on the records available then, that "only 5 or 6 were wounded," including one "Private Ferdinand Gerring of Carter's battalion, [who] later died of his wounds." Capt. William N. Robinson's official casualty report for the Battle of Palmetto, dated May 17, 1865, supports that estimate. Robinson, who commanded the first Confederates who encountered the Union advance, documented five wounded men by name and rank, four of them wounded "slightly" and one "Private F. Gerring" wounded "severely in shoulder." Combining Hunt's scholarly findings with Robinson's eyewitness report confirms Gerring's status as the last Confederate fatality of the Civil War. Hunt also conclusively documents the last Union fatality, Pvt. John J. Williams, making Palmito Ranch the site of the last Union and Confederate combat fatalities of the Civil War.[10]

Hunt painstakingly documents and describes the battlefield tactics of both Union and Confederate forces in May 1865, providing maps of the region, military posts, and terrain, complete with specific unit positions and movements during each phase of the battle. He employs scores of primary documents in that process and cites specific reports, statements, and transcripts from the post-battle Union court-martial of Lt. Col. Robert G. Morrison of the 34th Indiana Volunteer Infantry (in which the opposing commander, Texas Brig. Gen. John S. "Rip" Ford, also testified—a very unusual event in such cases). Despite Hunt's fine scholarship, his is not the final word on the historical significance of the Palmito Ranch Battlefield.[11]

The next chapter in documenting the little-known history of the Battle of Palmito Ranch came during the summer of 2008. The Texas Historical Commission (THC), having already participated in efforts to document the battlefield as early as 1963, began a new effort to do further research, supported by a first-of-its-kind grant from the Society of the Order of the Southern Cross (SOSC). Known for brick-and-mortar grants, the SOSC provided funding for academic research of the John S. Ford Papers at the Nita Stewart Haley Memorial Library and J. Evetts Haley History Center in Midland, Texas. Part of the Texas Confederate Museum Collection, the papers of "Rip" Ford (Texas Ranger, politician, secessionist, and commander of the Rio Grande Expeditionary Force during the Civil War) have long been under the care of the Texas Division of the United Daughters of the Confederacy. With the grant William A. McWhorter, at the time the THC's Military Sites Program coordinator, worked with historian Jody Edward Ginn to research the Ford Papers, a gold mine of primary documents related to the Palmito Ranch Battlefield.

In September 2009 and again in January 2010, Ginn and McWhorter traveled to Midland to the Haley History Center to research the recently acquired collection of daily ledgers kept by Ford as the commander of the Southern Division of the Western Subdistrict of Texas. There they met with J. Evetts Haley Jr., an officer of the SOSC and a descendant of a Confederate soldier who fought at the Battle of Palmito Ranch, who provided the authors with a tour and a fuller understanding of the Ford Papers' diaspora. Midland has turned out to be the final stop in what was a long and often uncertain journey for the Ford Papers, as they were moved frequently between various archives and storage facilities for almost a century, never becoming particularly well known or even accessible to researchers. Fewer than a handful of scholars have ever laid eyes on these documents, and until recently, no one had specifically mined them for information related to Palmito Ranch.[12]

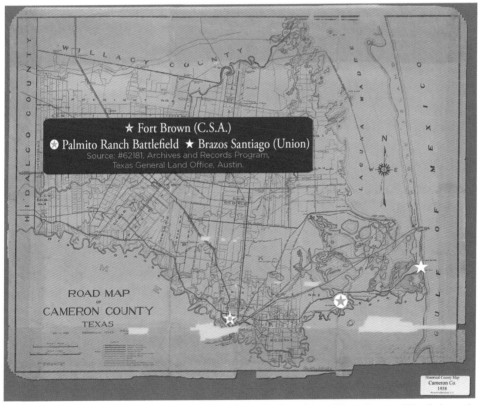

Cameron County Map (1938) annotated to show the location of Fort Brown (Confederate), Brazos Santiago (Union), and Palmito Ranch Battlefield (courtesy of the Texas General Land Office, source #62181).

Published works and the Ford Papers combine to illuminate the geographical relationship between Union forces on the coast, Fort Brown, and the battlefield. The battlefield's strategic position near the mouth of the Rio Grande along the Texas-Mexico border was no accident. As Richard B. McCaslin noted in this book's foreword, during the war the South's international boundary was critical to the Confederacy's pursuit of international recognition and economic viability. Recognizing the significance of Brownsville to the Confederacy and aware of French influence in Mexico under Napoleon III, the Union army made repeated attempts to seize control of South Texas during the war.[13]

Early in the Civil War, the Trans-Mississippi Department of the Confederacy learned to rely on Texas ports as an outlet for European cotton sales and the import of essential supplies. When Union ships sealed off seaports from Virginia to Texas, Confederate leaders transported cotton across the Rio Grande into neighboring Mexico, where locals aided smuggling efforts, and border towns, such as Matamoros in Mexico and Brownsville in Texas, prospered. Crews loaded the valuable cargo onto ships flying Mexican or European flags and carried it past the blockading Union flotillas.[14]

Protection of Texas ports and borders was of utmost concern to Confederate forces in the state. Although the Union had gained control of much of the Texas coast by January 1864, the occupation proved only temporary. In the summer of 1864, many Union troops began to withdraw from the Texas coast as the North focused more attention on campaigns back east. The Union forces that remained were limited to coastal defenses in support of blockading measures, one of which was on the northern tip of Brazos Island at Brazos Santiago Depot in relatively close proximity to Fort Brown.[15]

The resulting deployment of troops on both sides eventually led to not one but two battles at Palmito Ranch, the first in September 1864 and the second, better-known conflict in May 1865. The earlier clash was the larger of the two battles, and it involved the only documented incident of foreign troops engaging in actual combat on American soil during the Civil War. Like the second engagement, it was a victory for the Confederate Texans. Because of the May 1865 battle's place in history as the last land battle of the Civil War, this battle attained a special place in Texas lore, even if the site's name has differed among historians and heritage tourists, soldiers and local citizens. In *The Final Fury*, Philip Thomas Tucker contended that the spelling of "Palmito" as "Palmetto" and references to "Palmito Hill" or "Palmetto Hill" (rather than "Ranch") were the result of errors on the part of turn-of-the-twentieth-century scholars. Tucker used the spelling "Palmito" and disparaged the use of "Palmetto." However, numerous contemporary documents show that Confederate officers in their reports employed both spellings and that "Palmito [or Palmetto] Hill" was the "dominant terrain feature in the area" near which a substantial part of the 1865 battle occurred. This primary information should validate scholarly use of either spelling or any preference for referring to the location as "Hill" instead of "Ranch." With regard to spellings, the *Merriam-Webster Online Dictionary* explains that "palmetto" is a "modification" of the Spanish word "palmito." In the essential document collection on the Civil War, *War of the Rebellion: A Compilation of the Official Records of the Union and Confederate Armies*, Union officers Col. Theodore H. Barrett and Lt. Col. David Branson's reports are titled "May 11–14, 1865—Expedition from Brazos Santiago, Texas with Skirmishes (12th and 13th) at Palmetto Ranch and (13th) at White's Ranch." The spelling "Palmetto" shows that Union officers also preferred the Anglo form. Therefore, in the opinion of the authors, either spelling is acceptable.[16]

In accord with the site's contemporary and official designation, this book refers to the site as Palmito Ranch Battlefield, the Battle of Palmito Ranch, or Palmito Ranch Battlefield National Historic Landmark.

The debate over nomenclature has influenced historians' efforts to chronicle the battlefield but has also impacted the interpretive efforts of historic preservationists' placement of markers to commemorate the battlefield. During the Texas Independence Centennial observance in 1936, the Commission of Control for Texas Centennial Celebrations placed a granite monument at the battlefield with the inscription "Battle of Palmito Hill." In 1964, the THC, then called the Texas State Historical Survey Committee, placed a metal Tourist Information Marker with the same inscription. This metal marker was later stolen, replaced in 1990 by the THC with an official Texas Historical Marker inscribed "Battle of Palmito Ranch." The site's subsequent 1993 National Register of Historic Places and 1997 National Historic Landmark nominations referred to it as the "Palmito Ranch Battlefield." Archeological survey reports produced in 1999, 2001, and 2003 aided in documenting the battlefield.[17]

As archeologist Lila Rakoczy of the THC's Military Sites Program notes in an e-mail to McWhorter, "Battlefield (or conflict) archeology is immensely important to a more complete understanding of historic sites. . . . It is interlinked with the written historical documentation in what can be accomplished in accurately recording a field of battle." Battlefield preservation is important. "If you do not preserve battlefields, the rich information they contain will not survive to challenge or confirm the documentary record and accepted narrative of a battle." *Fields of Conflict: Battlefield Archaeology from the Roman Empire to the Korean War* by Douglas Scott, Lawrence Babits, and Charles M. Haecker, which includes a chapter on the Battle of Palmito Ranch, presents an understanding of how critical battlefield archeology can be to supporting or challenging the accepted written historic record.

In the fall of 2007, the US Fish and Wildlife Service, the majority landowner of the site today, provided THC staff with a tour of the portions of Palmito Hill under its stewardship. The purpose of the visit was for the THC to try to determine the exact location of the Washington, DC–based Civil War Trust's three-acre tract of land on the hill. This key meeting quickly developed into an opportunity to engage the public with a series of projects focused on research and interpretation, as well as awareness-building efforts such as Park Day. That critical step in 2007 set in motion more than a decade of cooperation between the THC and local and national stakeholders interested in saving the battlefield. Since then, multiple research and interpretation projects by the THC have kept the battlefield front and center for history lovers as the sesquicentennial of the battle approached in May 2015.

The THC works within and believes in the economic benefit of heritage tourism. In 1999, the THC commissioned a study (a collaboration between Rutgers University and the University of Texas at Austin) that quantified the economic contributions of historic preservation in Texas. "The 1999 study became one of the earliest and most comprehensive research efforts on this topic in the United States."[18] The THC updated the survey in 2015 and according to the state agency,

> Historic preservation is a major industry in Texas. The numbers tell the story: in 2013 preservation activities in Texas generated more than $4.6 billion of state gross domestic product (GDP) in Texas, and supported more than 79,000 Texas jobs. This produced significant net tax revenue for both state and local governments in Texas, equaling over $290 million annually. When viewed in cost-benefit terms, historic preservation is one of the best investments available today, for both developers and the public. Restored landmarks save materials and embodied energy from the landfill, while enhancing a sense of place and community pride. Preservation programs and initiatives are an important driving force for the Texas economy.[19]

Palmito Ranch Battlefield National Historic Landmark appears today much as it did in 1865. An open salt prairie dominates much of the site, which is broken only by occasional low, brush-covered hillocks and the dense chaparral that lines the Texas bank of the Rio Grande on the battlefield's southern boundary. The battlefield retains good integrity and conveys well to visitors the setting for the battle and its proximity to Texas' border with Mexico. Nevertheless, the battlefield is a nonrenewable cultural resource; if not protected, it can be lost forever. Continued preservation of the site and interpretation of the battlefield add to the nation's understanding of the Civil War through its multicultural and international aspects, as well as the unspoiled character of the landscape.

In the fall of 2014, the authors collaborated in writing a book that used the historical documentation within the Ford Papers to further document—and in some instances offer up new information to history enthusiasts—on both the May 1865 Battle of Palmito Ranch and the lesser-known First Battle of Palmito Ranch in September 1864, while intimately chronicling the extensive preservation effort of the battlefield by the THC and partners to save Palmito Ranch Battlefield.

1

John S. "Rip" Ford and Texas in the Civil War

In the years immediately prior to the Civil War, the United States was rife with conflict and controversy. Perhaps nowhere was the struggle more complex than in Texas. Some Texans supported the Union, but they were also concerned about political attacks on Southern institutions. Texas had been part of the United States just fifteen years when secessionists prevailed in a statewide election. Texas formally seceded on March 2, 1861, and became the seventh state to join the new Confederacy. Texas governor Sam Houston was against secession and struggled with loyalties to both his nation and his adopted state. His firm belief that Texas should remain in the Union cost him his office when he refused to take an oath of allegiance to the new national government.[1]

During the Civil War, Texans responded in impressive numbers and distinguished themselves in every major campaign from New Mexico to Pennsylvania. By the end of 1861, more than twenty-five thousand had joined the Confederate army. During the course of the war, nearly ninety thousand Texans served in the military. The National Park Service estimates that by war's end more than twenty thousand Hispanics, many of whom called Texas home, had fought in the Civil War nationwide. Leaders of the Texas forces included legendary figures such as John Bell Hood, Albert Sidney Johnston, John Bankhead Magruder, Patrick Cleburne, Santos Benavides, Ben McCulloch, and John S. Ford.[2]

Texas forces played prominent roles in celebrated Battles at Gettysburg, Antietam, Bull Run, Wilson's Creek, the Wilderness, Vicksburg, Corinth, Shiloh, Chickamauga, Glorieta Pass, Pea Ridge, Gaines's Mill, Franklin, and Mansfield, among others. In Texas during the war, Confederate and state forces repulsed Union invaders at Brownsville, Sabine Pass, Galveston, Corpus Christi, and Laredo and sustained naval bombardments in several coastal areas. They also fought Indians and border raiders, evaded Federal blockades, protected internal trade routes, and operated prisoner-of-war camps. Thousands more Texas civilians lent hearts and hands on the home front. While only one in every four antebellum-era Texas families owned slaves, African American slaves and their labor were a significant part of the Texas economy, especially in agricultural enterprises. During the war, major slaveholding portions of the state were not invaded, and slavery continued through the end of the war.[3]

The Trans-Mississippi Department of the Confederacy—which included Texas, Arkansas, and the Indian Territory—remained defiant through the end of the war, even after Gen. Robert E. Lee surrendered at Appomattox in April 1865. Nevertheless, most Confederate troops in the Trans-Mississippi formally surrendered on May 26, 1865. The Civil War came to a ceremonial end in Texas with the surrender of the Trans-Mississippi Department at Galveston on June 2, 1865, which Capt. Benjamin F. Sands of the US Navy noted as "the closing act of the Great Rebellion." Just a few weeks later, on June 19, Maj. Gen. Gordon Granger, commanding the District of Texas, from his headquarters in Galveston at the Osterman Building read General Order No. 3: "The people of Texas are informed that, in accordance with a proclamation from the executive of the United States, all slaves are free. This involves an absolute equality of personal rights and rights of property between former masters and slaves." With this notice, Reconstruction-era Texas began. This nationally significant event became known as Juneteenth and has grown into an annual worldwide celebration.[4]

In retrospect, Texas' secession and entry into the Civil War appear to have been foregone conclusions, but they were part of a process brought about by carefully planned political machinations, including the spread of fear and violence to undermine potential opposition. There were many Unionists in Texas at the time, not the least of whom was the incumbent governor, former US senator and former president of the Republic of Texas, Sam Houston. Nevertheless, Texas was dominated by the Southern Democratic Party machine, to the complete exclusion of Republicans and with only nominal participation by members of the national Democratic and Constitutional Union Parties. Despite the efforts of the latter two parties, secessionist candidates dominated the Texas delegation to the Democratic Party National Convention in 1860, thereby helping split the national ticket along regional lines and assuring victory for the Republican presidential candidate, Abraham Lincoln.[5]

Lincoln's election was the catalyst for secession that the Southern Democrats had been hoping for, as a grassroots movement sprang up spontaneously, with communities throughout the state holding mass meetings condemning Lincoln as a "Black Republican" and predicting war. Several notable state leaders, including famed Texas Ranger captain "Rip" Ford, took up the secession movement that had been initiated on the local level. Ford and his secessionist compatriots faced opposition from equally influential men who attempted to prevent disunion, with the help of perennial Texian hero Sam Houston, who urged restraint and careful consideration of the consequences of such actions, but to no avail. Secessionist leaders, including Ford, succeeded in holding a convention, passing an ordinance advocating for secession, and winning the referendum in support of that ordinance. However, while the ordinance did sever Texas from the Union, it did not join it to the not-yet-created Confederacy. That process began with sending delegates to join the meeting already under way in Montgomery, Alabama, to create the Confederacy and would be an issue that eventually divided the secessionists in Texas.[6]

Almost from the outset Ford, who was not a slave owner, had limited his support for secession to the reestablishment of the Republic of Texas instead of joining other Southern states in creating a new national government. Ford remained conflicted over the idea of fighting against the nation that his ancestors fought to create and sustain, as well as against friends and former comrades in arms. That internalized conflict likely influenced his decision to advocate for letting voters decide the issue in a referendum. Even before secession had been approved at the ballot box, Ford found himself charged with the state's defense. His success as a Texas Ranger commander established him as one of the leading military minds in Texas at the time, which resulted in his appointment to the Committee for Public Safety. Through the committee Ford guided the process of taking over federal property and replacing Union troops with state units. Ford was commissioned as a colonel by the state and assigned command over all posts along the Rio Grande from Laredo to Brownsville, which included the responsibility for securing federal property on behalf of the state and supervising the evacuation of Union troops, defending against "hostile invasions," and maintaining cordial relations with Mexico during that tumultuous period. Texan, and later Confederate, leaders recognized Brownsville's strategic value as an international port. Ford helped draft his own orders for that assignment, then personally recruited field commanders and six hundred volunteer troops, many of whom had previously served under him as Texas Rangers.[7]

On February 21, 1861, Ford peacefully took control of the post on Brazos Island at the mouth of the Rio Grande, which served as the army supply depot for Fort Brown and other posts farther upriver. In the process he seized twenty-one cannons and other military supplies to be used in the Texas war effort. Thanks to an agreement between the commander of Union military forces in Texas at the time, Brig. Gen. David E. Twiggs, and the intercession of other equally judicious Federal officers, all US forces agreed to surrender their posts and leave Texas peacefully. Ford oversaw that process in the Rio Grande Valley, from which the last Federal troops evacuated on March 21, 1861, and took pride in the fact that the process had concluded without bloodshed. The unexpected result of such a peaceful process was that state leaders saw no further need to maintain a substantial force in the region, and they reduced Ford's command accordingly. While many of Ford's colleagues and troops eventually sought more prominent assignments with the Confederate forces far away from Texas in the main theater of the war, Ford remained at home.[8]

Ford was appointed to command a new unit created by the Secession Convention called the Second Texas Mounted Rifles, which then transferred into Confederate service, a turn of events that led Ford to believe he was a Confederate colonel. The size and area of his command fluctuated during the first year of the war because of political maneuvering by various parties and changing leadership within the state's military command. Although initially commanded to move his troops north of Laredo and leave the defense of Fort Brown to an infantry unit, Ford remained in Brownsville. He split his command with John R. Baylor, who operated independently for the most part to the west of Laredo and launched an invasion of New Mexico. Meanwhile, Ford kept his attention focused on the lower Rio Grande and possible invasions by both Union troops and Mexican strongman (and perennial Texas adversary) Juan N. Cortina, which Ford believed were inevitable. Ford had his men reinforce Fort Brown's eroded earthwork defenses as he worked to maintain the peace between the Confederacy and Mexico, as well as among many Texans in the region. Although such efforts were not always accomplished without bloodshed, Ford's cordial relationship with Gen. Guadalupe García, who commanded Mexico's military forces on the Rio Grande, kept outbreaks of violence from spiraling out of control in the first years of the Civil War. And Ford's relations with Santiago Vidaurri, "strongman ruler of the northern Mexico states of Nuevo Leon and Tamaulipas," initially allowed the Confederates to keep cotton flowing across the Rio Grande and out to trade partners as far away as Europe.[9]

In the antebellum United States, cotton was an internationally traded commodity that drove the national economy. It was produced primarily in Southern states with slave labor and then sold to textile mills in the Northern states and Europe to be manufactured into marketable goods. Only one-fourth of Anglo-Texan farmers owned slaves, although those generated enough surplus cotton to turn the Lone Star State into the fifth-largest cotton-producing state in the Union by the late 1850s. Ford's work in the first year of the war helped Texas play that same role for the embattled Confederacy.[10]

However, Ford sometimes overplayed his hand in accommodating his Mexican associates, becoming entangled in revolutionary actions south of the border that disrupted the cross-border trade. After April 1862 he was removed from his command of the entire Rio Grande Valley, later termed the Western Subdistrict of Texas by the Confederate army, and lost his commission as a Confederate colonel, which he would never regain. Ford was assigned to enforce conscription out of San Antonio, a job that he pursued again in accordance with his own perspective and principles. He pragmatically recognized that Texas' frontier still required defense and therefore allowed those who wished to remain in Texas to enlist in state units rather the Confederate army, including men he knew to be Union sympathizers. Ford recognized that such men would be poor soldiers if forced into Confederate service and would be more likely to desert when the opportunity arose and provide information about Confederate military strength and movements to Union forces.[11]

Despite his sullied reputation at the national level of the Confederacy, Ford remained popular in Texas, where influential individuals and groups advocated for his promotion to brigadier general. State legislators, the Texas congressional delegation to the Confederacy, and many notable Texas business and government leaders lobbied on behalf of Ford, but Confederate leaders nonetheless refused to oblige them. However, when Union forces suddenly retook control of the Rio Grande border during November 1863 from Confederate commanders who had replaced Ford, many Texans, both in the general population and in state government, demanded his return to command of military forces in the region. Thanks to Lincoln's concerns over the cross-border cotton trade and his fears of an alliance between French troops in Mexico and the Confederacy, Ford was then restored to his former command with a "temporary" state brigadier general's commission. Ford would never again possess Confederate military credentials, but he returned to Brownsville in 1864 as a commander of state and Confederate troops.[12]

Gen. John B. Magruder, Confederate commander of the district that had included Texas, New Mexico, and Arizona since late 1862, ordered Ford to raise the Rio Grande Expeditionary Force and placed him in command with the express goal of driving the Union forces out of the Rio Grande Valley. The primary obstacles Ford faced during this period were lack of conscripts and volunteers, a severe lack of funding allocated for support of his command, and challenges to his authority by military rivals. Ford addressed the first by expanding his search beyond the standard pool of potential recruits by requesting soldiers previously assigned to frontier defense, accepting those outside draft age, recruiting men from across the Mexican border, and even soliciting deserters with the promise of pardons (which all of those who served under him at that time did receive). Often forced to scavenge whatever resources he could find, sometimes through questionable means, Ford struggled to keep his troops properly supplied and compensated for their service. Confiscated cotton sold through the cross-border trade routes was sometimes the best resource for such purposes.[13]

Ironically, the last land battle of the Civil War would be won for the Confederacy and Texas by a man who had lost his Confederate commission and led an army of castoffs. Ford used his popularity in Texas to create and supply the Rio Grande Expeditionary Force. With these men he won at Palmito Ranch not only in May 1865 but also in September 1864 against forces that included both Union troops and cavalrymen sent by his old nemesis, Cortina. In the 1864 battle, the fears of Federal leaders were confirmed when some French troops crossed the Rio Grande to fight for Ford. In sum, Ford's reputation and experience not only secured two victories for the Confederacy and Texas; they also defined how those battles were fought and how they were remembered.

2

The First Battle of Palmito Ranch, 1864

While underscoring the fact that Palmito Ranch was the site of the final land engagement between Union and Confederate forces in May 1865, the documents within the Ford Papers also reveal that the battle was actually the second at that location. The first occurred over the course of a week in September 1864 and is one of only two documented cases of foreign troops having engaged on one side or the other during the Civil War, the second instance being the May 1865 battle on the same site.[1]

Furthermore, the Ford Papers make it clear that it was no mere happenstance that those battles occurred at Palmito Ranch, as the Confederates regularly used the site as a forward outpost to defend Fort Brown and the city of Brownsville. From there the Confederates could protect the land-based approach along the military road between Fort Brown and the mouth of the Rio Grande at Boca Chica (the crossing to Brazos Santiago Depot, a Union post on Brazos Island) and monitor traffic traveling up the river. The Ford Papers also reinforce the notion that Ford's primary assigned objective was the protection of the cross-border cotton trade with Mexico, despite arguments by some scholars that the trade was minimal and therefore had little economic impact on the overall Confederate war effort. Finally, correspondence and reports in the Ford Papers demonstrate that Confederate Texan soldiers (excepting deserters) remained optimistic and willing to fight and die for their cause despite news of mounting Confederate losses and Lee's surrender at Appomattox at a time when many, if not most, Southerners already considered their cause to be lost.[2]

This assessment is supported by a substantial number of records found in the Ford Papers, including after-action reports by several commanders who participated in the September 1864 battle and numerous standard field reports and returns (official company records that included a variety of data, such as current manpower, supply status/needs, and brief accounts of events and actions taken) submitted by commanders stationed at the site throughout 1864 and 1865. The site is alternatively referred to as "Palmito Rancho," "Rancho del Palmito," "Palmetto Ranch," "Palmetto Rancho," "Camp Palmetto," "Camp Palmetto Rancho," "Camp Rancho del Palmito," "Camp del Palmito," "Station Rancho del Palmeto," and "Station Palmito Rancho."[3]

These records indicate that at least one company was always stationed at Palmito Ranch from approximately July 1864, after Ford's Rio Grande Expeditionary Force chased the Union army off the Texas mainland for the second time during the war, until May 1865. During that time, and during the battles in September 1864 and May 1865, Confederate troops stationed at the ranch exploited its position adjacent to the military road (sometimes referred to as "Bocha Road" or "River Road") between Brownsville and Boca Chica. Its placement on a bend of the north bank of the Rio Grande was pivotal to successfully monitor traffic along the only two thoroughfares that provided access to Fort Brown from the Gulf of Mexico. While traffic along the road rarely consisted of anyone other than Confederate troops and a handful of recognizable locals, boat traffic up and down the river appears to have been fairly steady, keeping Confederate pickets busy detaining, searching, and sometimes commandeering sailing and steam vessels. The ranch's location on an elevated stretch of the riverbank also allowed the Confederates to monitor the movements of both Mexican bandits and troops, particularly those under the command of Ford's frequent nemesis, Juan N. Cortina. Its position approximately halfway between Fort Brown and Brazos Island also made it a convenient spot from which to send pickets to observe the activities of the Union army at Brazos Santiago Depot and quickly return with intelligence reports.[4]

A prolonged engagement between Confederate and Union troops (supplemented by Mexican forces under the command of Cortina) in 1864 lasted several days. The opposing forces moved back and forth across a ten-plus mile area, from near Boca Chica to the far side of the Palmito Ranch area, finally culminating in a pitched battle at Palmito Ranch during September 6–11.

Because the site was approximately midway between the Union troops at Brazos Santiago Depot and Ford's command at Fort Brown, it became the place of engagement between those forces on more than one occasion. Confederate field and after-action reports from September 1864 describe the site as being ten miles above the mouth of the Rio Grande and provide key details on the first battle to have occurred there. Union and Mexican forces successfully used chaparral in the area as cover, and the Confederates used the sand hills as cover for their own attack to regain control of the site. In November, Capt. Theophilus G. Anderson specifically reported deliberately stationing his pickets so that it would be "impossible to surprise me [him] from the mouth of the river, or Brazos Island." Ford and his field commanders recognized the site's overall strategic value, and they maintained a presence there from July 1864 until May 1865, when the war finally came to a close in Texas.[5]

Beginning in August 1864, field commander Lt. Col. Daniel Showalter of the 4th Cavalry Regiment, Arizona Brigade, reported that his troops had been engaged in "several skirmishes," resulting in the capture of up to a dozen Union prisoners of war and "a good steamer called the *Ark of New Orleans*." In the wake of these engagements, Showalter set up his headquarters at "Rancho del Palmito." On September 5, Showalter reported from "Camp Palmetto" that Mexican "Colonel" Juan N. Cortina was attempting to restrict all traffic along the Rio Grande. He requested permission from Ford to use the *Ark* to challenge Cortina and perhaps provoke him into a fight. He did not make the request out of wanton aggressiveness; he had been trying to obtain needed forage and supplies for his troops and their horses, a process that Cortina's actions were impeding.[6]

Showalter's request turned out to be unnecessary, as the boat he sent upriver was able to pass through "without any trouble." That same day, he also reported that Cortina had "about 300 men with two pieces of artillery" and that "another force of 300" with one piece of artillery was approaching that morning. Showalter admitted that he had no evidence to determine the Mexicans' intentions at the time of the report, but he suspected that they were planning to cross the Rio Grande into Texas. He also noted that Union forces at Brazos Santiago Depot had reassembled "with approximately 1000 Negro Infantry."[7] Two days later, Showalter reported that "the Mexicans have opened on our camp and are now shelling us," and he suspected "the Yankees" would join them shortly.[8]

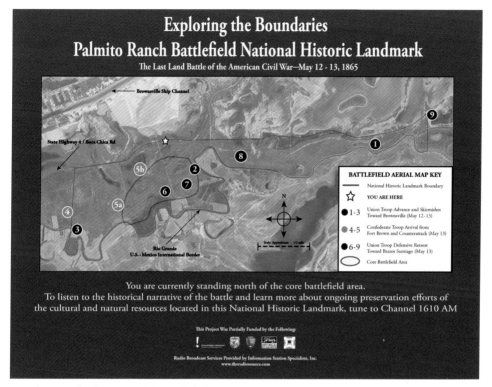

Aerial map of Palmito Ranch Battlefield (courtesy of the Texas Historical Commission).

Showalter confirmed in his after-action report from Rancho del Palmito that Mexican forces attacked him on September 6, 1864, with artillery from the Mexican side of the Rio Grande, and they were soon joined by Union cavalry and artillery from Brazos Santiago. Showalter noted that Cortina's position across the river was beyond the range of small-arms fire and that his own troops had no means of crossing the river to attack the Mexicans. Nevertheless, the Confederate Texans held their position until 1:00 p.m., when Union troops arrived and attacked them from the east "with about 500 cavalry and 2 pieces of artillery." [9]

By that point Showalter's Confederates, caught in the crossfire between the Mexicans to the south and the Union troops to the east, "fell back in the direction of Brownsville seven miles, where the advance of the enemy was checked." Showalter later reported that on September 9, three days later, his rested troopers reinforced Lt. Col. George H. Giddings's Texas cavalry battalion in attacking "the enemy four miles above and forced him back to this point [Palmito]." On September 11, they "drove the enemy from this point . . . the Yankees retiring to Brazos Island and the Mexicans who had joined them to the Mexican side of the river."[10] This was not the first time during the Civil War that Cortina's men had crossed the Rio Grande to attack Ford's troops, but it was the first documented case of them engaging in combat against the Confederates in concert with Union forces. Showalter further reported that the Confederates then reoccupied Palmito Ranch, at which point he and other commanders began composing and submitting their reports of the engagement.[11]

While some scholars have noted that Cortina's artillery aided the Union during that conflict by firing from across the river, no published account other than Ford's memoir has acknowledged that Mexican troops actually crossed the river and joined with Union forces in active combat against the Confederates. The Ford Papers also contain a letter dated September 17, 1864, from Agapito Longoria, mayor of Matamoros, to Ford, requesting that he release Mexican soldiers held as prisoners of war to Longoria as a courtesy. Ford's prompt and polite reply denying the mayor's request stated that the Union commanders involved had claimed the Mexican soldiers as their own, making their release subject to existing Union-Confederate prisoner-exchange protocols. The Union officers likely took that step to provide their Mexican/Cortinista allies with a plausible legal defense for crossing the recognized international border to attack an undeclared enemy, a clear violation of international law regarding warfare.[12]

Giddings also submitted an after-action report for his unit's involvement in the fighting on September 9, "in front of and above Palmetto Ranch," though he makes no mention of Showalter's unit having been involved. Giddings stated that he was notified at approximately 3:30 p.m. that his companies led by Captains William N. Robinson, Sanders, and J. M. Onins (with Onins in command as the senior officer) were encircling the Union forces positioned at Morton's Ranch. Giddings then instructed his men to attack the Union forces in their center as soon as Onins initiated an attack on the rear and Capt. R. W. Carr engaged them from the front. He also noted that Capt. José del Refugio Benavides's cavalry company supported the charge on the Union center.[13]

Giddings's after-action report described having been notified that a company of Union troops had positioned themselves inside what appeared to be an impassable ravine, but the Federals apparently retreated before his

advance party arrived. Giddings's men soon found a crossing over the ravine, while troops under the command of Benavides crossed two hundred
yards to their right. With half of his men yet to cross, Giddings was fired on
by a combined party of Union and Mexican soldiers who were hidden in
the chaparral to his left. Giddings also noted that Captain Carr's company
drove the enemy skirmishers from his front, and in the process many of
them took refuge in the chaparral just in front of Benavides, who pursued
them in their flight for three-quarters of a mile through the brush.[14]

Giddings further described how a "number of squads of horsemen and
infantry" struggled "up the hill" where they had artillery positioned. When
Giddings found himself without the necessary manpower to charge the
center of the enemy forces, he ordered his men to fall back and "secure their
horses in the chaparral and advance on foot to the edge of [the] prairie,"
where they remained under heavy fire for two hours. When the firing to
their right ceased, they "mounted [their] horses and rode to the edge of
[the] Prairie and fired a volley at the enemy who replied very faintly. [They]
then retraced [their] steps to the [San] Martin Ranch." The only reported
Confederate casualty from that engagement was a private, J. J. Oliver, who
"was killed while we were crossing the ravine when the enemy first opened
upon us from the chaparrals in front." None of the commanders provided a detailed analysis of the terrain surrounding Palmito Ranch, but the
notes documenting the advantages provided by hills, chaparral, and ravines
demonstrate that they recognized that these features could be used to their
military advantage, both in active combat and in routine defensive and surveillance activities.[15]

Giddings boasted that the Confederate soldiers "rushed into the chaparral
at full speed" and that the "Yankees and the Mexicans were swept away like
chaff before the wind." He added that Captain Carr's company had "driven
the enemy skirmishers from his front[,] many of whom took refuge in the
chaparral immediately in front of Benavides's command," although "they
did not succeed . . . to check his progress." Both Giddings's and Benavides's
troops proceeded to a position approximately five hundred yards from the
main Union battery. Giddings witnessed several squads of cavalry and infantry "struggling up the hill towards the Union artillery positions," at which
point he gave the order to open fire, to which the Union forces responded
with "a discharge of shell and round shot from their battery and a shower of
sharpshooter and cannon balls which seemed to come from every conceiv-
able direction."[16]

Also on September 9, Colonel Ford sent a letter to Capt. A. Veron, commander of the French naval forces stationed at Bagdad, Mexico, just south of Boca Chica, notifying him that "there is no doubt, but that a treaty was concluded between the United States and Cortina" and that he believed they were preparing to "march upon Brownsville." He further noted that there were "six pieces of artillery" firing on Confederate troops from the Mexican side of the river. Ford claimed to have a note from Cortina alleging his justification for the attack, stating that the Confederates were in league with the French imperial forces in Mexico. He asked Veron to send "a force up the river and co-operate with us" and gave the French commander authorization to enter Confederate territory with his troops for as long as necessary "to pursue and chastise Cortina."[17]

Hostilities continued on September 10, with Captain Robinson reporting the second Confederate fatality of the ongoing conflict on that date. Although he provided no details concerning the action or circumstances involved, Robinson reported that an unnamed second lieutenant was killed in action "at a Rancho," a report that corresponds with a note on Captain Carr's September 1864 field return documenting the death of 2nd Lt. S. P. Travis of Robinson's company.[18] Capt. Wiley H. D. Carrington submitted several reports and a return to Ford that are mostly undated but specifically relate to several engagements near Palmetto Ranch beginning on September 9. Carrington also documented the death of Pvt. J. J. Oliver, a member of his company, noting that with the exception of "the loss of said Oliver," the cavalry charge that day "upon Yankees and Mexicans strongly posted in chaparral . . . was successful." He also noted that a photograph of his men was taken at the time and that all prisoners of war had been transferred to Houston. Captain Carrington composed multiple letters to Ford over the course of several days of fighting, providing both reports on the action and tactical suggestions. In a letter to Ford that appears to have been written on September 10, Carrington reported having approached Palmito Ranch that morning to find "20 or 25 Mexican and Yankee pickets exactly where we left them yesterday." He stated that his men "skirmished with them for half an hour and fell back a few hundred yards hoping to draw them out but they would not come out." He also reported hearing "heavy firing this morning at the mouth of the river area."[19]

In an apparently subsequent communication, Carrington apologized for the "meagerness" of his reports, explaining that he did not have adequate stationery supplies. He then suggested that Ford send three hundred men

to attack "Palmetto Ranch," as he thought that would be sufficient to capture the enemy troops currently stationed there, and added that a Mexican
was watching his unit's movements "very minutely" from across the river.
He then repeated his description of how he tried to "draw the enemy out"
the night before and that he did not otherwise have sufficient manpower to
make a direct attack on the enemy position.[20]

The final report from Captain Carrington stated that while there were
no "Mexicans or Yankees this side [west/southwest] of Col. Showalter's old
camp [Palmito Ranch]," there was "an encampment at that place." He reported that pickets spotted him while on reconnaissance approximately
one mile from Palmito Ranch and "fired signal guns along the river to the
cabins in which Col. Showalter [had been] encamped." He reaffirmed his
unit's inadequate troop strength for a direct assault on the camp, reporting
that he had twenty-five fewer men, a loss that was further exacerbated by
"broken down horses and diarrhea." He concluded with a note that he had
placed pickets near the San Martin Ranch and that the "Yankee pickets now
come two hundred yards this way." While Carrington was apparently doing
what he could to stall the advance of the Federals and Cortinistas, he was
unable to push them back without reinforcements as of early September
11, 1864.[21]

Carrington's pleas for assistance would not go unheeded. Ford sent an
order placing forces near San Martin Ranch on September 10, and Giddings
reported back on his unit's progress toward Palmito Ranch on September
11. Giddings described how one hundred of his men "moved down near
Palmetto Ranch" to support Captains Robinson and Sanders but were unable to "make the enemy show their strength." Giddings surmised that the
joint Union/Cortinista forces were unlikely to relinquish Palmito Ranch
without a fight and noted that Cortina's troops again fired artillery rounds
at them from across the river for about half an hour on the evening of
September 10. Giddings's artillerymen returned "a few shots" across the
river, and he sent pickets within a mile of Palmito Ranch. Giddings sent
Lieutenant Nash's company eight miles up the "Isabel Road," where they
encountered "48 Yanks." He declared that although he remained cautious,
he believed that they could "whip" the enemy forces.[22]

On September 11, Giddings engaged the joint Union/Cortinista units,
estimating that they had between four hundred and five hundred infantrymen, two hundred cavalry, and two cannons on the ground and another on a steamship nearby. The Union/Cortinista troops opened fire with

their artillery and then attempted a cavalry charge, which Giddings's men repulsed. Giddings then began relieving his pickets and begged Ford for replacement horses because his were exhausted and "constantly given out." Giddings also requested that Ford send him paper on which to continue writing his reports, a request that apparently was fulfilled that same day.[23]

By 8:30 a.m. on September 11, Giddings had "driven the enemy from" their position at Palmito Ranch, putting Confederate forces back in place at that "field Camp." Giddings's main force at that point consisted of only 150 men, but they were in pursuit of the Union forces along the "Bocha Road." A French steamer/gunboat was patrolling the river at the same time. Giddings once again reported that their horses were "really exhausted," requesting that one hundred reinforcements be sent up the "Isabel Road" and report back to him daily. Giddings noted that there were "no casualties on our side," but his men were exhausted from "constant duty + constant fighting."[24]

By 7:30 that same evening, Giddings was reporting that enemy prisoners and horses were being brought back to his headquarters at "Palmetto Ranch." He noted that his horses were so "broken down" that his men were unable to keep up the pursuit that night, but he added that they would "push through tomorrow." Giddings sent Captain Brady to communicate with and buy corn and supplies from Veron, the French naval commander at Bagdad, by way of a chartered boat. Veron had apparently put the Union commanders on notice that if Cortina turned out to be with them, they must turn him over or the French naval fleet would "shell them off the Island." Giddings closed his report by stating that "the Isabel Road . . . is safe" and he is confident that his forces would be able to push all the way to the mouth of the Rio Grande the following day.[25]

Giddings's assessment of the circumstances proved correct, as Captain Carrington reported at 10:45 a.m. on September 12 from "Camp Palmetto Rancho" that all of the "Yankees are inside Brazos Santiago, except about 60 cavalry on the sand hills" near Boca Chica. However, he also noted that Union boats were moving up and down the river. This turned out to be no problem for the Confederates because the French navy was also patrolling the river all the way up to Brownsville, with a total of five boats. While "Camp Palmetto" continued to serve as the Confederate headquarters, Giddings had moved down to the "White House" (presumably White's Ranch, a small settlement east of Palmito Ranch) just after 12:30 p.m. that day to secure the corn and supplies he had requested the day before.

Maj. Gen. Thomas F. Drayton, the new Confederate district commander who arrived at "Camp Palmetto" by 4:00 p.m. on September 12, gave Ford permission to cross over to the Mexican bank of the river "if necessary, but not otherwise."[26]

By September 14, all Union forces were at Brazos Santiago Depot, some of them boarding boats presumably bound for New Orleans. Confederate field reports indicated all was quiet, and Giddings began sending troops back toward Brownsville, although he did leave two hundred men under Major Cavanaugh stationed at Camp Palmetto Rancho. Two days later, on September 16, some Cortinistas who had been transported back to the Mexican bank of the Rio Grande by Union boats fired several shots at Confederate pickets near Camp Palmetto Rancho, but Giddings reported that the brief encounter was "nothing serious." Routine operations and problems replaced the "continuous fighting" of the preceding days, including communications with Veron regarding Cortina's disposition, the inspection and sale of the *Ark of New Orleans*, and issues involving insubordination by an officer. They also began the process of prisoner exchange with the Union commanders. All was quiet on the Rio Grande Valley front.[27]

Although exact troop strength and casualty estimates are difficult to pinpoint, it is evident that the First Battle of Palmito Ranch involved larger forces on both sides than the second and that it lasted three times as long as the later engagement. Even though the 1864 battle proved to be over by September 12, the Confederate commanders remained vigilant, keeping a close eye on the Union forces at Brazos Santiago and the Cortinistas across the river in the subsequent days and months. Palmito Ranch continued to serve as the forward observation post for the Confederate troops in Brownsville, not only throughout the remainder of the year but also until Union forces attempted one more advance toward Fort Brown in May 1865. Needless to say, the Confederates posted at Palmito Ranch knew of that advance well before the inexperienced and arrogant Union colonel, Theodore Barrett, realized his strategic and personal miscalculations regarding the steadfast Confederate troopers defending the Rio Grande Valley.[28]

While far more research is necessary to fully understand this battle and the forces that fought there, the work to date demonstrates the forgotten battlefield's significance and how it adds to the nation's understanding of the Civil War through its military, multicultural, and international aspects. As significant as the first battle is, its successor has been far more researched, resulting in interpretation and commemoration efforts since the 1930s.

3

The Second Battle of Palmito Ranch, 1865

"Last Land Battle of the Civil War"

Although the Union maintained armed forces at Brazos Santiago, and the Confederacy, at Fort Brown, by May 1865 the leaders of both armies had realized that the Civil War was essentially over and that continued fighting in Texas would do little to change the final outcome. Until the Battle of Palmito Ranch began on May 11, 1865, "both sides honored an informal truce agreement negotiated about two months earlier between Union Maj. Gen. Lew Wallace, Confederate Brig. Gen. James E. Slaughter, and Texas Brig. Gen. John S. (Rip) Ford."[1]

On May 11, the informal truce was broken when Union commander Col. Theodore H. Barrett ordered a force that consisted of African American soldiers of the 62nd Infantry, US Colored Troops and white troopers from the 2nd Texas Cavalry (dismounted), pro-Union Texans who had joined the Federal army, to make a landing at Boca Chica and march on Fort Brown. Early on the morning of May 12, Lt. Col. David Branson ordered his troops to surround White's Ranch, a small settlement east of Palmito Ranch, in hopes of capturing the post and its Confederate garrison. The Federals discovered that the outpost had been deserted one or two days before they arrived. The Imperial Mexican Army was much more sympathetic to the Confederate cause. Later that morning persons on the Mexican side of the Rio Grande spotted the Union detachment and promptly brought the concealed soldiers to the attention of the Confederates. When the Union soldiers started for Palmito Ranch, they had to skirmish most of the way with Giddings's battalion of Confederate cavalry under the command of Capt. William N. Robinson, driving them from their camp by noon. By this time the Union force had reached San Martin Ranch, west of Palmito Ranch; Ford sent a message to Robinson urging that his force hold its ground and promising that he would bring reinforcements as soon as possible.[2]

After the brief skirmishing west of Palmito Ranch, Union troops retired to what was referred to during the Civil War, and still is 150 years later, as Palmito Hill to rest and feed their animals. At approximately 3:00 p.m., a reinforced Confederate force appeared and the Union force considered its position on Palmito Hill to be indefensible, so Branson led his troops back to White's Ranch for the night. At White's Ranch, he sent a message to Barrett requesting additional support. At daybreak the next morning (May 13), Branson and his men were joined at White's Ranch by two hundred men of the 34th Indiana Volunteer Infantry (also known as the Morton Rifles), under the command of Lt. Col. Robert G. Morrison. Barrett subsequently joined these troops, assumed command of the enlarged Federal force, and pushed west toward Brownsville.[3]

By about 4:00 p.m. on May 13, Ford and his reinforcements concluded their long march from Fort Brown, having reached a point near San Martin Ranch. The Union army was in sight, although not yet aware of the Confederates' presence. Ford issued directions for a two-pronged attack. Colonel Barrett and the Union troops abruptly found themselves facing a largely reinforced Confederate army, possessing several cannons (which the Union force did not have), advancing toward them not only in the front but also on their right flank, in an attempt to gain their rear. The Union soldiers prepared for the imminent attack by forming an oblique skirmish line, extending from the Rio Grande on the Union left and stretching north to cover their line of retreat. The heaviest fighting of the battle commenced. When the Confederate cavalry charged, it became apparent that too few Union skirmishers had deployed to mount an effective challenge to the approaching Confederate troops.[4]

Ford's flanking maneuver eventually overwhelmed the Union skirmishers left to cover the withdrawal of the two Union infantry regiments from the Palmito Ranch area. Their retreat was hastened by the fact that the northern wing of the Confederate flanking maneuver threatened to cut

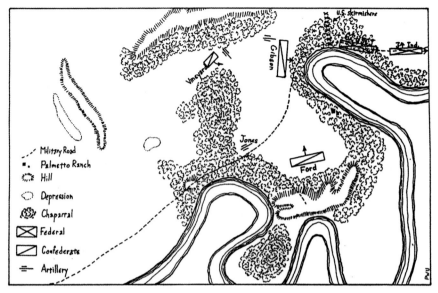

Escape of Barrett's command, Battle of Palmito Ranch (from Hunt, *The Last Battle of the Civil War*, 108).

off the escape route for the Union force at a choke point above Palmito Ranch, where the Rio Grande bends northward. Although the majority of the Union forces made it out of the Palmito Ranch area, several smaller units were lost. As the Union force retreated eastward, the 62nd Infantry provided a series of delaying actions that held off the pursuing Confederate forces until the bulk of the Union forces reached the relative safety of its post at Brazos Santiago.[5]

The Union forces were driven back because of Colonel Barrett's poor leadership, the Confederates' effective flanking maneuver, and the Confederate Texan soldiers' willingness to fight and die for their cause despite news of mounting Confederate losses. The Confederates fought effectively, defending their home state, and by day's end approximately 270 Confederate cavalrymen and 30 artillerymen (reinforced by 120 cavalrymen after driving the Union soldiers into a full retreat) defeated 450 Union infantrymen, 50 dismounted cavalrymen, and 2 officers. The two-day engagement left "2 killed, 6 wounded (including 2 prisoners), 102 prisoners (not wounded), and 2 missing."[6] The Confederates pursued the Union troops northward out of the battlefield area and then eastward toward the coast for roughly seven to eight miles. The Union troops were driven to Cobb's

Ranch about two miles from Boca Chica, where Ford ordered his troops to halt. The day after the battle, representatives from both the Confederate and Union forces met at the courthouse in Brownsville.

The Confederates were under the impression that there was a truce still in effect in the lower Rio Grande. Thus, they were surprised by the Union advance toward Brownsville on May 12 because just a few weeks earlier, Confederates thought that the Union troops were evacuating to New Orleans. On April 25, Ford received a report from Capt. Thomas C. Cater, whose company was stationed at "Palmito Rancho." That report indicated that Union forces at Brazos Santiago were "making a move . . . in the direction of Corpus Christi," with steamship runs occurring "daily." The next day Ford's adjutant, Lt. Edward Duggan, was forwarded a report from Confederate pickets by Captain Robinson from his station at "Camp Palimita." The pickets reported that two ships had left the island outpost on April 25, and the post flag had not been hoisted nor the traditional evening gun fired for the past three days. In light of these activities and the previous truce, the Confederates' confusion on witnessing the westward advance of Union troops a couple of weeks later was understandable.[7]

The Ford Papers also debunk a long-standing myth regarding the make-up of Ford's forces in South Texas. For generations, scholars have repeated the claim that Ford's Rio Grande Expeditionary Force consisted almost entirely of "old men and young boys." However, several muster rolls in the Ford Papers provide the names and dates of birth of several hundred of Ford's troopers, only a handful of whom were outside the draft age. These rolls document the men's status as conscripts and the diversity of those men serving the Confederacy. They included Tejanos, American Indians, Anglos, Portuguese, Irish, Germans, Africans, and Danes.[8]

Union commanders defeated that May quickly realized that someone would have to take the fall for their failure and began political maneuvering to protect themselves and their units from blame. Capt. Abraham M. Templer even wrote an unprecedented letter to Ford, dated May 17, 1865, requesting that he provide "a certificate of my conduct and the conduct of [my] men . . . in the late engagement near Palmetto Ranch," because he feared that "there may [be] some doubt arise against us [for] not doing our duty." He added a postscript requesting that Ford send the desired certificate by way of Bagdad, Mexico, presumably to ensure that other Union commanders did not intercept it. Ford later testified, during the Union court-martial of Lieutenant Colonel Morrison, that Templer and his men "did their duty well [and] stood as long as they could" in what was a tactically hopeless situation.[9]

Some historians have also raised the issue of mass desertions among Ford's men on learning of Gen. Robert E. Lee's surrender at Appomattox a few weeks before the May 1865 battle. The Ford Papers give no indication of such occurrences, with most desertions shown to have been in December 1864.[10] As documented by historian and author Jeffrey William Hunt, Ford quickly assembled more than 300 cavalrymen and artillerymen at virtually a moment's notice (with another 120 joining him a day later), even though the bulk of his forces had been scattered up and down the lower Rio Grande. This was possible because the Confederate commanders, believing that a truce was in effect, had dispersed their troops so they would have an easier time finding forage for their horses. The fact that Ford's troops fought so bravely and aggressively also undermines the notion that Lee's surrender had damaged morale in Confederate Texas. While in retrospect historians have most often pointed to Lee's surrender as the end of the war for all practical purposes, such a teleological assessment held no bearing on the minds of Confederate soldiers in South Texas in May 1865.[11]

Civil War enthusiasts will likely continue to quibble over inconsequential minutiae to assert their region's and ancestors' significance in the Civil War. However, the historical significance of Palmito Ranch as the site of the last land battle of the Civil War has been well established by recent scholarship, and many documents in the more recently accessible Ford Papers underscore and support that assessment. Scholars and critics have long questioned many of Ford's assertions regarding the battle. However, primary-source documents in both the Ford Papers and the records of the court-martial of Lt. Col. Robert G. Morrison support most of Ford's own statements and writings regarding Confederate casualties during these engagements, thereby debunking claims that he underreported his own losses. The Ford Papers also help establish the site as the location where the last two (of more than six hundred thousand) fatalities during the Civil War were inflicted.[12]

Additionally, the Ford Papers show that the site of the battle, along with the makeup of the terrain (including Palmito Hill, the highest point in the area, along with smaller sand hills, ravines, and dense chaparral thickets dispersed throughout the area) and its close proximity to a sharp bend in the Rio Grande, made it a strategically valuable position to mid-nineteenth-century military forces. Those geographical features, which contributed to Palmito Ranch becoming the site of two confrontations between Union and Confederate forces, had provided the Confederate troops with a forward encampment from which to observe and report on Union activities at Brazos Santiago Depot since July 1864.[13]

Research into the second battle originally brought attention to Palmito Ranch as the site of the last engagement of the Civil War, but it also revealed information regarding the first battle. Thus, the site has been found to be of historical strategic military value with the distinction as the only location where foreign troops actively participated in combat during the Civil War.

The Palmito Ranch house was the spot where the most troops were concentrated over the longest period of time. Union, Mexican, and Confederate troops dug in there at various times during the first battle (including the time when the Rebels were being continuously bombarded by Cortina's artillery across the river). Since the house and adjoining structures were burned by the Union forces during the last battle and apparently never rebuilt, the site may very well serve as a prime location for future archeological studies.

4

From Battlefield to National Historic Landmark

The Battle of Palmito Ranch in May 1865 represents more than the final land action of the Civil War. The engagement is an important part of the complex story about how the war ended in the field, not at the conference table. While the battle in no way changed the outcome of the war, its historic significance is undeniable, not only to Texans but to a growing number of historians and Civil War enthusiasts during the recent sesquicentennial observation. The position of a Confederate force in Brownsville during the Civil War was as much for military protection as economic security. In response to the Union blockade of the Confederacy's coastlines, Southerners transported cotton grown west of the Mississippi through this part of Texas, across the border and into Mexico, and then from ports on the Gulf Coast of Mexico to European textile mills. In sum, the site may be seen as the final link in the chain of events that began at Fort Sumter, South Carolina. Thus, preservation of the site and interpretation of the battlefield add to the nation's more complete understanding of the Civil War through its multicultural and international elements.[1]

The history of how the location of the last land battle of the Civil War became a revered historic site in Texas is not much different from how many Civil War battlefields have become a part of our shared history. The story begins shortly after the last shots were fired on May 13, 1865. Most Confederate troops in Texas were officially surrendered on May 26, with the remnants of the Trans-Mississippi Department surrendering on June 2. Union troops then occupied Brownsville, and their garrison post in South Texas during the war, Brazos Santiago, was abandoned shortly thereafter. As the nation moved away from the war and the former Confederate States were readmitted into the Union, including Texas in 1870, the war's lasting impact on Texas remained, and in the early twentieth century interpretation of the battle's story began to be set in stone monuments.[2]

An exhaustive discussion of how memory compares with the reality of historic events lies outside the scope of this book, but a discussion of how the Battle of Palmito Ranch has been interpreted through historical markers and documented in academic historical research should be included. Preservation of the battlefield and its history exists because the site clearly connected to Texans' persistent Southern identity and the "Lost Cause" movement of the latter part of the nineteenth and early twentieth centuries, which sought to bolster camaraderie among Southern veterans and restore the honor of fallen Confederate soldiers. In an effort to make sense of the tremendous loss of life, materials, and treasure caused by the Civil War, its veterans looked within. Beginning in the 1880s, Civil War veterans across the nation, Union and Confederate alike, wished to observe the camaraderie and memory of their war experiences and sacrifices. Due to the small number of participants on both sides, historical documentation of reunions at the Battle of Palmito Ranch has yet to be uncovered. However, documentation of how the battlefield has been marked dates back nearly eight decades. Through the actions of private heritage preservation groups and the efforts of the State of Texas—in celebrating its own centennial in 1936—the battlefield has been commemorated with a series of memorial markers since the mid-1930s.[3]

Cross-border transit of cotton was absolutely critical to the Confederacy's economy during the Civil War. Brownsville's strategic position along the Confederacy's only international border during the war arguably brought wealth to the community thanks to the key crop of cotton. How fitting it is that the postwar success of Brownsville and the Rio Grande Valley also evolved because of agriculture. The construction of the St. Louis, Brownsville, and Mexico Railroad in 1904 brought an influx of Northerners to purchase lands for citrus, cotton, sorghum, melons, and other agriculture opportunities. During the early twentieth century, the region witnessed a large-scale transformation; farmers cleared land and trenched the soil for irrigation systems, while communities laid roads to support the growing citrus farming industry of today's Rio Grande Valley.[4]

In addition, Brownsville benefited in the century after the Civil War thanks to continued federal government involvement in Cameron County, as major projects, such as the Depression-era Works Progress Administration's construction of the port of Brownsville, brought economic development to the region. After Texas rejoined the Union, Fort Brown continued to serve the nation as a US military post until 1944, when the last garrison left shortly before the end of World War II. The site is now located on the campus of Texas Southmost College next to the University of Texas Rio Grande Valley. The campus borders the Rio Grande, and one of the region's leading employers, the Department of Homeland Security, patrols the area through the US Border Patrol and Customs Administration.[5]

Notably, the economic growth and continued government presence in Cameron County over the past 150 years have not demonstrably impacted the battlefield, and much of its historic integrity survives. Palmito Ranch Battlefield National Historic Landmark (NHL) is located approximately twelve miles east of Brownsville in far southeastern Cameron County along a portion of the Rio Grande. The primary vehicular access from Brownsville to the battlefield is State Highway 4, which lies on the battlefield's northern side. Perpendicular to the highway, Palmito Hill Road (a gravel road owned by Cameron County) provides access to the core battlefield area and the public portion of the road's terminus at Palmito Hill. The boundaries of Palmito Ranch Battlefield NHL encompass 5,991 acres, while the core battlefield, site of the most intense fighting, is slightly less than 1,000 acres.[6]

The topography of the battlefield is relatively flat, with sporadic clay dunes thick with vegetation, called lomas; shallow brackish bays; a salt prairie; and a subtropical climate with temperatures ranging from fifty to ninety-four degrees Fahrenheit. Since the end of the war—as they did before the war—local landowners have used minor portions of Palmito Ranch Battlefield for cattle ranching. These factors and the proximity of the battlefield to the Gulf Coast made the site almost unsuitable for large-scale agricultural production, limiting the type of development that would have negatively impacted the battlefield.[7]

The lack of large-scale development helped preserve a diverse array of wildlife found throughout the battlefield today. In 1979, to protect the tremendous biological diversity of this remote region, the US Fish and Wildlife Service established the Lower Rio Grande Valley National Wildlife Refuge. A part of the service's South Texas Refuge Complex, the refuge is a wildlife corridor that follows the Rio Grande along the last 275 river miles, connecting isolated tracts of land managed by private landowners, nonprofit orga-nizations, the State of Texas, and two other national wildlife refuges, Laguna Atascosa and Santa Ana. Within this NHL, several privately owned tracts of land adjoin the Lower Rio Grande Valley National Wildlife Refuge. The resulting conservation of local habitat for the area's fauna and flora greatly aided the preservation of a nearly pristine Civil War–era battlefield.[8]

Along with Palmito Ranch Battlefield NHL's historic location, appear-ance, ambience, and association, the memory of the battle has remained strong among those who treasure Texas history. During the Great Depres-sion of the 1930s, while the economic circumstances in Texas gave little reason to celebrate, many citizens of the Lone Star State commemorated the centennial of Texas independence in a big way. Through two huge ex-positions in Dallas and Fort Worth, the dedication of a towering monu-ment at the Texas Revolution–era Battle of San Jacinto and new memorial museums, community centers, statues, monuments, and historical markers throughout the state, Texas and federal officials spent millions of dollars entertaining and educating Texans and visitors from around the world. Among the most enduring legacies of this extraordinary commemorative effort are the historical markers and monuments that can still be found in nearly all of Texas' 254 counties. They represent an unprecedented effort to document the stories of Texas along highways and little-known back roads to educate the public about the history of Texas. In the 1930s, the arrival of these granite and bronze objects and their subsequent dedication ceremo-nies became causes to celebrate and display community pride. Today, the majority of the more than eleven hundred historical markers and mon-uments placed in 1936 remain sources of information and inspiration to new generations each day.[9]

During the 1936 Texas Centennial, a gray granite marker with a bronze star and wreath attached was installed at the battle site that noted the "Last Battle of the Civil War." In July of that year, the Commission of Control for Texas Centennial Celebrations placed the "Battle of Palmito Hill" marker near the core battlefield area along Highway 4.[10]

The Texas Centennial Marker's inscription reads,[11]

At This Site
The last battle of the Civil War, known as Palmito Hill, was fought by Confederate Troops under Colonel John S. (Rip) Ford and Union Forces on May 13, 1865; 34 days after Lee's surrender at Appomattox.

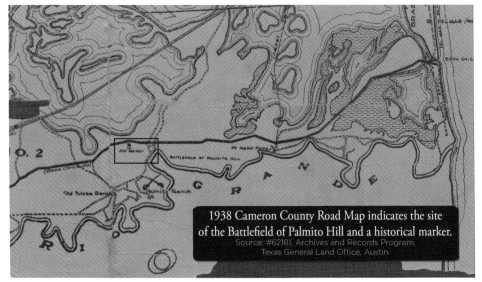

1938 Cameron County Road Map indicates the site of the Battlefield of Palmito Hill and a historical marker. Source: #62181, Archives and Records Program, Texas General Land Office, Austin.

Cameron County map (1938) annotated to illustrate the location of the first State of Texas monument at the battlefield (courtesy of the Texas General Land Office, source #62181).

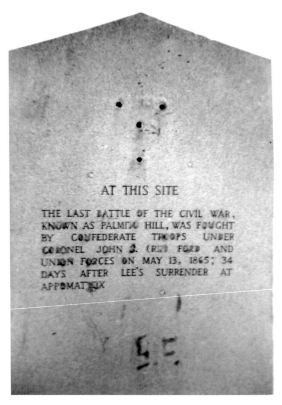

AT THIS SITE

THE LAST BATTLE OF THE CIVIL WAR, KNOWN AS PALMITO HILL, WAS FOUGHT BY CONFEDERATE TROOPS UNDER COLONEL JOHN S. (RIP FORD AND UNION FORCES ON MAY 13, 1865; 34 DAYS AFTER LEE'S SURRENDER AT APPOMATTOX

With its bronze wreath and star removed by vandals, the original 1936 Texas Centennial Marker for the Battle of Palmito Hill (courtesy of the Texas Historical Commission).

This official attempt by the state to mark the property is most likely not the first time the battlefield was commemorated in stone. Shortly before the authors began work on this book, the Texas Department of Transportation shared a photograph of another 1930s-era stone monument placed at the battlefield to the THC. The square granite monument has a bronze plaque. The image, found in the Transportation Department's scrapbook for the Brownsville District, has a photo-processing stamp dated December 1936, and in an effort to determine the provenance of this marker, the authors searched through a number of resources. This research bore fruit, as a photograph of the marker accompanied an article about the Battle of Palmito Ranch in the April 12, 1936, issue of the Brownsville *Herald*. Further research at the Texas State Library and Archives provided additional information. This first known granite marker commemorating the battlefield measured 3.5 feet high, 2 feet wide, and 1 foot thick, and was placed by the Daughters of the American Revolution, likely sometime between 1931 and 1936.[12]

Monument marking Battle of Palmito Hill
Last battle of Civil War - May 13, 1865.
On Highway #4 - 12 miles East of Brownsville.

Daughters of the American Revolution monument (ca. 1936) along State Highway 4 in Cameron County. The caption reads, "Monument marking Battle of Palmito Hill; Last battle of Civil War—May 13, 1865. On Hwy #4—12 miles East of Brownsville." The photograph is from the Brownsville District album and has a photo-processing stamp on the back dated December 1936 (Raapp3NImage Library 3HistoryPharr District, District Views c1936PHR_25b) (courtesy of the Texas Department of Transportation Media Production Division, Austin, Texas).

Thus, decades before the commemoration of the centennial of the Civil War (1961–1965), the placing of two granite markers at the site clearly indicates that Palmito Ranch Battlefield was already firmly positioned in Texas history as worthy of being remembered. Heritage tourists are now able to visit the site and remember the soldiers who had fought the closing act of the Civil War in deep South Texas.

More than two decades later, on the eve of the centennial of the Civil War in 1957, the US House of Representatives passed Joint Resolution 253, authorizing all state governors to create their own Civil War Centennial Commissions for organizing and directing observations of key dates within their borders. Texas governor Price Daniel established the Texas Civil War Centennial Commission (TCWCC) by executive order on December 14, 1959. During the first years of the centennial the TCWCC generally met quarterly to discuss upcoming projects and events. At these meetings, the Texas State Historical Survey Committee (in 1973 renamed the Texas Historical Commission) provided vital administrative support to the TCWCC and helped plan preservation projects and commemorations. On July 12, 1963, the duties given to the TCWCC transferred by gubernatorial order to the Texas State Historical Survey Committee, which then established the Texas Civil War Centennial Advisory Committee. The new committee held its first meeting on August 17, 1963, in Austin.[13]

Between 1961 and 1965, the committee accomplished several projects: marking veterans' graves and acquiring Texas soldiers' service records held on microfilm by the National Archives and Records Administration; compiling a chronology of wartime events; dedicating new state buildings, such as the Texas State Library and Archives building and the Texas Supreme Court building, designated as a Confederate memorial by constitutional amendment; erecting out-of-state historical monuments on battlefields; and publishing two small books, *Texas in the Civil War* and *Texas at Vicksburg*. In addition to these ambitious projects, the committee placed granite and metal historical markers across Texas.[14]

In 1964 and 1965, the Texas Civil War Centennial Advisory Committee knew that it had a unique commemorative opportunity: the final centennial observance of a Civil War battle would occur in deep South Texas. The two markers already placed provided, at best, only limited on-site interpretation of the site. To add to the interpretation at the historic battlefield, the committee, in cooperation with the Texas Tourist Marker Committee, erected a Tourist Information Marker on January 11, 1964, alongside one of the previous granite monuments on Highway 4 in far eastern Cameron County.[15]

The "Battle of Palmito Hill" Tourist Information Marker, the eighth produced in a special series of twenty-two markers, was made of cast aluminum by Sewah Studios.[16] The marker's inscription reads,

> The last land engagement of the war between the states was fought near this site on May 12–13, 1865, thirty-four days after General Robert E. Lee surrendered the Army of Northern Virginia at Appomattox. It was not until June 2 that the Trans-Mississippi Department of which Texas was a part finally surrendered.
>
> On the eve of the battle, Colonel Theodore H. Barrett commanded several hundred Federal troops on Brazos Island twelve miles to the east. The Confederates under General James E. Slaughter occupied

Tourist Information Marker for the Battle of Palmito Hill (1964) (courtesy of University of Texas Rio Grande Valley, Brownsville).

Fort Brown at Brownsville twelve miles to the west. With him was Colonel John S. (Rip) Ford, whose troops had forced the Federals out of Fort Brown in July 1864.

Ordered to recapture Fort Brown, Lieutenant Colonel David Branson with 300 men advanced by night from Brazos Island via Boca Chica Pass and the pickets near here on the afternoon of May 12. The skirmishing that followed favored the Federals.

Colonel Barrett reinforced Branson's forces with 200 men on May 13. Assuming command, Barrett renewed the march to Fort Brown. Confederate Cavalry held the Federals in check until Colonel Ford arrived in midafternoon with reinforcements. The Federal skirmish line extended south to north.

Colonel Ford quickly made his troop dispositions. His artillery was advanced and ordered to fire on the northern end of the Federal line. The supporting Confederate Cavalry opened with rifle fire and then charged the same sector. Meantime the Confederate right charged the southern end of the Federal line and captured a portion of the 34th Indiana Infantry.

Barrett ordered a retreat, halting twice before coming within protective range of the Brazos Island guns. There were no Confederate fatalities reported. The Union forces lost four officers and 111 men killed, wounded or missing.

A Memorial to Texans Who Served the Confederacy.

Intended to add to the existing interpretation at the battlefield, placed the year before the centennial anniversary of the May 1865 Battle of Palmito Ranch, the marker would soon be the lone interpretive piece at the battlefield for more than a quarter of a century.

Due to damage to the 1936 marker's inscription and removal of its bronze wreath and star, noted as early as 1958, the Centennial Marker was removed to the Texas Highway Department's Brownsville garage on Highway 281 when the Tourist Information Marker was placed in 1964. The other granite marker at the battlefield by this time was in no shape to offer visitors additional information about the battle. By 1964, the once pristine granite marker was lying knocked over in a gully, with its bronze plaque pried off. Correspondence from the Cameron County Historical Survey Committee and the Texas State Historical Survey Committee in June 1964 indicated a desire to see the DAR granite marker repaired when it was also removed to the local Texas Highway Department garage. Further corre-

Dedication of the Tourist Information Marker for the Battle of
Palmito Hill. Left to right: Menton Murray, Texas state representative;
John Ben Shepherd, president of the Texas State Historical Survey
Committee; Jim Bates, Texas state senator; and Louis V. Boling,
chairman of the Hidalgo County Historical Survey Committee
(courtesy of the Texas Historical Commission).

spondence between the two committees in 1964 and early 1965 indicated a
desire to salvage the Centennial Marker and place it back at the battlefield
in time for the centennial commemoration of the Battle of Palmito Ranch
in May 1965.[17] This did not happen, however; correspondence indicated
that the Centennial Marker was too badly damaged to be salvaged. Sadly,
the ultimate fate of both markers, after they were moved to the garage in
Brownsville, remains unknown at the time of this book's publication. The
fate of the Centennial Marker, while unfortunate, is not unique to Cameron

County. Vandalism, erosion, weathering, and even new construction developments have left many such markers across Texas marred, pockmarked, overgrown, toppled, lost, and forgotten.[18]

For the next quarter of a century, the Tourist Information Marker remained the only on-site interpretation of the battlefield until it also fell victim to intentional damage. In 1989, Cameron County Historical Commission communications to the THC note that the Tourist Information Marker was badly vandalized. The commission's report indicated that the marker showed damage "consistent with the likely use of a large vehicle to ram it." The marker was bent, knocked off its metal pole, and even had some bullet holes. That summer, members of the commission worked to straighten the marker's pole and set the marker upright. Their hard work was in vain, as further correspondence with the THC noted the marker had been stolen, likely in June or July of that year. With the theft of the 1964 marker, the battlefield lost its last commemorative interpretive marker. Fortunately, the battlefield would not have to wait long, because in August 1989 the commission applied for a replacement marker.[19]

In early 1990, an Official Texas Historical Marker cast by the Southwell Company of San Antonio, measuring twenty-seven by forty-two inches, noticeably smaller than the out-of-production Tourist Information Markers, was shipped to Brownsville for placement.[20] The new marker, most likely affixed by the Cameron County Historical Commission to a concrete backing, added protection from future vandalism and theft. The inscription on the marker reads,

Battle of Palmito Ranch
The last land engagement of the Civil War was fought near this site on May 12–13, 1865, thirty-four days after Robert E. Lee surrendered at Appomattox.
Col. Theodore H. Barrett commanded Federal troops on Brazos Island 12 miles to the east. The Confederates occupied Fort Brown 12 miles to the west, commanded by Gen. James E. Slaughter and Col. John S. (Rip) Ford, whose troops had captured Fort Brown from the Federals in 1864.
Ordered to recapture the fort, Lt. Col. David Branson and 300 men advanced from Brazos Island. They won a skirmish with Confederate pickets on May 12. Barrett reinforced Branson's troops with 200 men on May 13 and renewed the march to Fort Brown. Confederate cavalry held the Federals in check until Ford arrived with reinforcements

that afternoon. Ford's artillery advanced and fired on the northern end of the Federal line while the cavalry charged. The Confederate right charged the southern end of the Federal line and captured part of the Union infantry. Barrett ordered a retreat toward the US position on Brazos Island.

While the Confederates reported no fatalities in the Battle of Palmito Ranch, the Union forces reported four officers and 111 men killed, wounded or missing.[21]

The 1990 replacement marker remained the battlefield's lone piece of on-site interpretation for the next twenty-one years. It served as the first undertaking during the decade that included a series of academic efforts

Replacement Texas Historical Marker (1990) affixed to a concrete backing shaped to resemble a 1936 Texas Centennial Marker (courtesy of the Texas Historical Commission).

toward a more complete understanding of the battlefield's history and significance. On June 23, 1993, the National Park Service listed the Battle of Palmito Ranch, under Criterion A for historic association, in the National Register of Historic Places. The nomination focused on the May 1865 engagement's significance as the example that "uniquely represents the crucial role of deep south Texas to the Confederacy's pursuit of international recognition and economic viability during the American Civil War." A review of the documents associated with the battlefield's 1993 National Register nomination indicate that in their comments on the site's nomination as a National Historic Landmark, US Fish and Wildlife officials declared that they "looked forward to cooperation with the THC toward the identification and preservation of historic resources in the Rio Grande Valley." The two agencies did indeed cooperate in this endeavor.[22]

Following the battlefield's elevation to NHL status in 1997, a series of reports by both the National Park Service and local preservationists—hoping to add to the written scholarship on the battlefield's history and to improve on the NHL's delineation of the battlefield's boundaries—produced two key reports. *Battlefield Core Area Identification Report* appeared in 1999, and *Cultural Resource Research, Identification and Documentation Resource Reconnaissance Survey* was completed in 2002.

Time has revealed the significance of the Battle of Palmito Ranch within the historical narrative of both Texas and the United States, as evidenced by the markers and academic and archeological surveys of the site. In the decades following the Civil War, the Battle of Palmito Ranch moved from a footnote in arguably the seminal event in US history during the 1800s— the Civil War—to an academically, copiously documented historic site with national significance related to the cross-border cotton trade during the war. State Historical Markers and a National Register of Historic Places listing, as well as battlefield studies, have aided in preserving the history of the battle and, to a significant degree, the physical boundaries of the battlefield.[23]

5

Park Day Gets the Ball Rolling

Efforts such as historical markers, archeological surveys, and National Register nominations have each advanced the documentation of the Battle of Palmito Ranch. Building on these efforts in preservation, since 2007 the THC and a growing alliance of regional and national partners has succeeded in increasing the awareness and interpretation of the battlefield.

In September 2007, John L. Nau III, chairman of the THC, a noted Civil War history enthusiast, preservationist of Texas history, and a successful businessman, instructed THC staff to reach out to the Civil War Trust (CWT) regarding the battlefield. The CWT is the nation's largest nonprofit organization with the mission of preserving America's most significant Civil War battlefields. It protects what its members consider to be hallowed ground and educates the public about the vital roles the battlefields played in the course of American history. Thanks to private donations and influential members, the CWT has preserved thousands of acres across the country, including a small portion of the site of the Battle of Palmito Ranch.[1]

By 2007, the approaching sesquicentennial of the Civil War (2011–2015) offered academic and public historians across the nation the opportunity to reflect on many topics of interest. For the THC, the primary interest centered on what forms of interpretation existed regarding sites in Texas associated with the war and how these sites have been presented to the public. It was often discovered that stories of minorities, including those of pro-Union Texans, were underrepresented. By attempting a more inclusive telling of Texas Civil War history, THC historians could honor the Texas mystique and expand information about the war. In 2008, the state agency undertook this task as it embraced the opportunity of telling more stories through enhancing the interpretations at its newly acquired state historic sites related to the Civil War. The same opportunity was presented to the CWT in regard to the Battle of Palmito Ranch. As of November 2001, the CWT owned a three-acre parcel of the battlefield atop Palmito Hill, but its offices are located in Washington, DC Any THC site visit would have to be self-guided.[2] Wanting to make the most out of this first tour of the battlefield, the THC reached out to another local battlefield landowner, the US Fish and Wildlife Service's South Texas Refuge Complex, to secure permission to walk tracts adjacent to the CWT's three acres.[3]

On November 13, 2007, THC historians traveled to Alamo, Texas, headquarters of the South Texas Refuge Complex. The complex comprises the Lower Rio Grande Valley National Wildlife Refuge (LRGV Refuge), the Laguna Atascosa and Santa Ana National Wildlife Refuges, and many acres of private lands that form a corridor running southward along the Rio Grande. The LRGV Refuge, which encompasses 80 percent of the Palmito Ranch Battlefield NHL, is the sector that is involved with the battlefield. The LRGV Refuge was established in 1979 under the authority of the 1956 Fish and Wildlife Act and the Migratory Bird Treaty Act as a long-term program of acquiring lands to protect and restore the unique biodiversity of the refuge. The combination of climate, geology, topography, vegetation, and wildlife within creates a highly varied biological diversity found nowhere else in Texas or the United States.[4]

From Alamo, Nancy Brown, public outreach specialist, and her LRGV Refuge colleagues led the THC historians in a tour of the battlefield. A long day of walking through brush and repeated stops for map reading resulted in the THC staff gaining a good understanding of the battlefield's landscape. After a day on-site, it was clear how well the battlefield had retained its physical integrity, thanks in large part to the environmental conservation efforts of the US Fish and Wildlife Service.[5]

In addition to touring the battlefield and gaining an effective understanding of its landscape, THC representatives making the site visit produced two key results. First, that 2007 face-to-face meeting between the THC and US Fish and Wildlife Service resulted in the discovery of an earlier cooperative effort between the CWT, the US Fish and Wildlife Service, and

Texas Historical Commission's site visit with the US Fish and Wildlife Service to Palmito Ranch Battlefield (2007) (courtesy of the Texas Historical Commission).

the National Park Service to create a visitor center at the battlefield. Second, THC had contacted the US Fish and Wildlife Service in October 2007 about co-hosting a Park Day. The battlefield tour ended in an agreement between the two groups to partner the following spring with the CWT and local stakeholders to host the first Park Day at Palmito Ranch Battlefield NHL. This initial visit led to several projects and a beneficial relationship between the THC and the US Fish and Wildlife Service that has lasted past the observance of the battle's sesquicentennial in May 2015 to the present.

Intrigued by the information the US Fish and Wildlife Service had shared about past joint efforts to create a visitor center at the battlefield,

THC historians went to work to gain a better understanding of this past preservation effort. Documents on file at the THC showed that as early as 1999, the CWT had wanted to partner with the THC, the National Park Service, and other local groups to acquire approximately 342.2 acres of the core battlefield area for preservation, to be administered by the National Park Service. Further review of documents and correspondence associated with the Battle of Palmito Ranch indicates that this large-scale plan quickly dropped to a significantly smaller number of acres because of the cost of the land. In response, the CWT initiated a scaled-down acquisition effort focused on a different portion of the battlefield. In this second effort, the CWT considered the purchase of seventeen acres on the crest of Palmito Hill. Here the consortium of preservationist partners working on the land acquisition through the CWT proposed that a viewing platform be built to overlook the core battlefield area in a northwesterly direction. Accessible from the county-owned Palmito Hill Road, the seventeen-acre tract was large enough to support parking facilities, placed behind (or south) of the hill's crest and outside the battlefield's vista. The area was considered large enough by the CWT, the National Park Service, and local historic preservationists to support visitor activities to the battlefield while preserving the natural setting of the property. This proposed undertaking would have ensured continued preservation of the impressive vista of the core battlefield area while exposing visitors to the integrity, feeling, and associative context of the NHL location. However, a lack of local landowner participation resulted in the CWT purchasing only three acres atop Palmito Hill. An analysis of the correspondence between the consortium of preservationist partners indicates that cost of the land led to the purchase of fewer acres.[6]

The parcel acquired for preservation is located within the core battlefield area, and the CWT's stewardship of the property has aided Palmito Ranch Battlefield NHL's retention of historic integrity. A National Park Service letter to the THC in June 2001 accompanied a new report that stated, "[The three acre] tract [known as Palmito Hill] provides a key and historic vantage point or overlook of the battle site." The report, *Resource Reconnaissance Study for the Palmito Ranch Battlefield*, outlined the battlefield's boundaries and provided helpful documentation for THC historians rapidly learning about the battlefield. The report noted an earlier source, the Civil War Sites Advisory Commission's 1993 *Report on the Nation's Civil War Battlefields*, which itself lists the Battle of Palmito Ranch as "the most important site associated with the International Interpretive theme of the

Civil War" and gave the Texas battlefield a rating of "B," on a scale of "A" (most significant to the course of the war) to "D" (relatively insignificant to the outcome of the war).[7]

The CWT purchased the land, hoping to encourage introduction of an ambitious congressional bill to authorize the National Park Service to allow nearby Palo Alto Battlefield National Historical Park (then National Historic Site), which interprets the Mexican-American War, to administer the three acres as a subunit, hosting on-site interpretive services for visitors. After CWT's donation of the land to the National Park Service, Palo Alto Battlefield's boundary would change to include what was to be called the "Palmito Ranch Battlefield Unit." With the US Fish and Wildlife Service's ownership of hundreds of acres of property near the CWT tract, a significant portion of the overall battlefield would now be managed by two agencies of the Department of the Interior.[8]

Through the efforts of THC chairman Nau; Frank Yturria, a local preservationist and THC commissioner at the time; and other stakeholders, agreements were sought to meet the CWT's desired outcome for the three-acre tract. The consortium sought the assistance of US senator Kay Bailey Hutchison to achieve the goal, and correspondence from the spring and summer of 2001 indicates that the effort was moving forward. However, the goal was not achieved, most likely due to the national emergency caused by the September 11, 2001, terrorist attacks. Thus, the three acres on Palmito Hill have remained in the possession of the CWT, and neither the consortium nor any other stakeholder has continued to pursue the option of having the National Park Service administer the Palmito Ranch Battlefield Unit.[9]

Thus, while the battlefield looked much as it did during the war, by 2007 there was still just one historical marker on-site. Furthermore, no one organization or governmental agency officially was in charge of interpretation at the battlefield. By 2008, scholarly and preservation organizations that focus on the Civil War were making preparations to observe and commemorate the forthcoming sesquicentennial of the Civil War: the Austin and Houston Civil War Round Tables, the Hood's Texas Brigade Association Re-Activated, the Sons of Confederate Veterans, the Sons of Union Veterans, and the United Daughters of the Confederacy. These groups and the general public asked for feedback about the THC plans for observance of the sesquicentennial, which essentially meant, "What did the THC have the capacity to do to observe the sesquicentennial?" By 2008, the THC had reinstituted its successful Texas Civil War Monuments Program run through the Military Sites Program and the Friends of the Texas Historical Commission. In addition, the agency had a nationally respected Historical Marker Program, a handful of state historic sites related to the Civil War, and a strong relationship with county historical commissions. Together these would ultimately provide the opportunity to address the little-known stories of the Battles of Palmito Ranch during the following decade.

Since 1996, Park Day has provided an opportunity to historic preservationists across the nation to coordinate their own annual projects at some of the most well-known and the most obscure Civil War battlefields. An annual event, Park Day is sponsored by the CWT and seeks volunteers to clean and repair the grounds of Civil War battlefields. At each site, volunteers receive a free T-shirt and patches, and they have the opportunity to hear historians interpret the battle. Under the leadership and with the support of THC chairman Nau, the agency hosted the first two Park Days in Texas on April 5, 2008. By co-hosting Park Day with the Jefferson and Cameron County Historical Commissions at the two Civil War battlefields on the same day, halfway across the state from each other, the THC initiated a unique effort in engaging heritage tourism at the neglected Palmito Ranch Battlefield NHL and the newly acquired historic site at Sabine Pass.[10]

Before Park Day, on January 1, 2008, the Texas legislature transferred the fifty-eight-acre Sabine Pass Battleground State Historic Site in Jefferson County and seventeen other state historic sites from the Texas Parks and Wildlife Department to the THC for management and rehabilitation.[11] Classified as a Priority II, Class B battlefield by the Civil War Sites Advisory Commission, the Sabine Pass site interprets both an earlier 1862 battle and the more well-known September 8, 1863, Battle of Sabine Pass. During the latter, Lt. Richard "Dick" Dowling and his forty-six men at Fort Griffin fought a Union amphibious attack on Sabine Pass, a primary Texas port for shipments of supplies that were vital to the South's war effort. To disrupt the viable Confederate trade route through Mexico, President Abraham Lincoln sent a naval force to capture Sabine Pass, near the Louisiana border, and from there began an occupation of portions of Texas. The only Confederate line of defense at this battle was a few dozen artillerists manning six cannons inside Fort Griffin. In a battle lasting less than an hour, Dowling and his men destroyed two gunboats, inflicting significant casualties and capturing nearly 350 prisoners. The successful defense by the outnumbered Texan defenders resulted in one of the most lopsided victories of the entire war. Thanks to their efforts, area ports escaped capture, and Union forces never penetrated the Texas interior.[12]

At Sabine Pass, Park Day activities centered around a workshop on cleaning historical markers and a public-speaking event that highlighted the site's significance. The CWT's support of the battlefield helped attract a large number of preservationists that day, and by February 2009 Texas history lovers founded the Friends of Sabine Pass Battleground to further support the rehabilitation and interpretation of the site. Sadly, Hurricane Ike made landfall in late 2008 and caused immense destruction in its wake, which kept the site closed until September 2009. But true to form, the CWT brought national attention to damage at the site by placing Sabine Pass Battleground State Historic Site in its timely report, *History under Siege: A Guide to America's Most Endangered Civil War Battlefields.* Within the year the THC and local preservationists had the park restored and open to heritage tourism.[13]

Far to the south in Cameron County, two new partners joined the THC-led effort for the first Park Day at Palmito Ranch Battlefield NHL. In February 2008, Chair Larry Lof and the Cameron County Historical Commission agreed to serve as an official local sponsor to help the THC with coordination of the day's events. About this time, the THC reached out to the National Park Service to help promote Park Day. Mary Kralovec, then superintendent of Palo Alto Battlefield National Historical Park (at the time National Historic Site), and Douglas Murphy, chief of operations/interpretation, demonstrated eagerness to work with the THC to provide information from their agency concerning the battlefield.[14]

While William McWhorter coordinated Park Day at Sabine Pass Battleground, Bob Brinkman, the THC's Marker Program coordinator, led Palmito Ranch Battlefield NHL's first-ever Park Day. In 2008, and even now, there is no interpretive center or manned presence at the site. To give the public attending Park Day a place to assemble for the day's events, Superintendent Kralovec opened up her park's visitor center for registration. After orientation, Park Day attendees convoyed toward Palmito Ranch Battlefield NHL; waiting on-site was staff from the US Fish and Wildlife Service with the National Historic Landmark plaque in hand to mark the historical significance of the site.[15]

Park Day events at Palmito Ranch Battlefield NHL included a historical marker cleaning workshop, trash pickup, and historic battlefield oration. In addition, in what has turned out to be a unique spin on Park Day, US

Palmito Ranch Battlefield National Historic Landmark plaque displayed by the US Fish and Wildlife Service at the first Park Day, 2008 (courtesy of the Texas Historical Commission).

The first Park Day at Palmito Ranch Battlefield, 2008 (courtesy of the Texas Historical Commission).

Fish and Wildlife Service staff joined the battlefield historians and imparted information on their agency's undertakings to preserve the area's flora and fauna. At each Park Day since, the THC has asked US Fish and Wildlife staff to speak to the attendees about their agency's preservation efforts. Visitors today can truly envision what the battlefield looked like to the Union and Confederate soldiers during both battles at Palmito Ranch in 1864 and 1865. In May 2008 the THC met with the US Fish and Wildlife Service, the Cameron County Historical Commission, and the National Park Service in Brownsville to discuss additional interpretive possibilities for Palmito Ranch Battlefield NHL.[16]

Before the THC could participate in more on-site interpretive projects and host follow-up Park Days, staff needed to conduct further research into the battle to provide accurate historical interpretation to the public. During the summer of 2008 the Friends of the Texas Historical Commission applied for its first grant for projects at the battlefield and received a grant from the Society of the Order of the Southern Cross for academic research in the Ford Papers. The group hired academic historian Jody E. Ginn to work along with William McWhorter to conduct the research. Ginn's research and writing in 2009–2010 not only provided the THC with a concise, professional report but also inspired this book.[17]

What followed this first grant was a phenomenal response from foundations, government agencies, and private individuals who supported ongoing preservation efforts associated with the Palmito Ranch Battlefield NHL. Eight additional grants and gifts were awarded that increased the capacity for the THC's Military Sites Program to enhance the on-site interpretation and preserve the history of the battlefield.[18]

On March 17, 2009, THC staff traveled once more to Brownsville to meet with the National Park Service to discuss increasing the interpretive efforts at Palmito Ranch Battlefield NHL. This meeting laid the groundwork for a proposed future project: an interpretive viewing platform, located within the core battlefield area. LRGV Refuge manager Bryan Winton entered the picture at this meeting. A former US Marine, Winton from day one brought a great passion for preserving the natural beauty of South Texas wildlife and for the historic preservation of cultural resources.

Within a month of this meeting, Katherine Faz, then the community planner for the National Park Service's Rivers, Trails, and Conservation Assistance Program, Texas Division, who had been working with the THC on unrelated projects, reached out to McWhorter with yet another new opportunity for the stakeholders. The National Park Service American Battlefield Protection Program (ABPP), in concert with Superintendent Kralovec, finalized details regarding an upcoming special training session in South Texas later that summer. The National Park Service extended invitations to battlefield site managers and collections managers who would benefit from a two-day training session on battlefield research and mapping, elements of the effective battlefield plan, and funding.[19] The classroom-style Battlefield Preservation and Collection Management workshop held on June 16–17, 2009, at the University of Texas at Brownsville/Texas Southmost College included a field trip to the battlefield site. The National Park Service proposed that the THC assist with the site visit to the Palmito Ranch Battlefield.[20]

In 2009, the CWT's nationwide date for Park Day, April 4, fell on a busy day for historic preservation organizations, which were that year hosting multiple events across Texas. When the THC inquired about setting a date for Park Day 2009 at Palmito Ranch Battlefield NHL, Superintendent Kralovec and her staff at Palo Alto Battlefield were busy preparing for the upcoming June battlefield preservation workshop with National Park Service ABPP staff from Washington, DC This workshop provided the perfect opportunity to hold the battlefield's second Park Day and engage a new audience.[21]

On that hot, June day in South Texas, the National Park Service and the THC provided workshop attendees with an understanding of the battlefield's history, including a briefing on how traditional military analysis, known as KOCOA (Key terrain, Observation and fields of fire, Cover and concealment, Obstacles, and Avenues of approach and retreat) might be applied in future efforts to increase the battlefield's documentation. The US Fish and Wildlife Service joined the group that day and provided attendees with a firm grasp of the local terrain and habitat. This first, and so far only, Battlefield Preservation and Collection Management workshop held at Palmito Ranch Battlefield NHL provided the THC with the opportunity to hold Park Day for a second consecutive year, and the free Civil War Trust Park Day T-shirts were a big hit with participants. What started the ball rolling in 2008 was now truly building momentum for interest in the battlefield.[22]

Later that year, another pivotal player responsible for helping the battlefield entered the stage. On November 16, 2009, Wilson Bourgeois, a historian who was at that time unknown to the THC, made his way to the Texas

State Capitol in Austin. A resident of Brownsville in Cameron County, Bourgeois had recently been the subject of a Rio Grande Valley area media release as a burgeoning historian, specializing in the history of the Battle of Palmito Ranch. The staff of the Texas Civil War Museum of Fort Worth, having read an article about Bourgeois, invited him to serve as their key-note speaker at a ceremony held in honor of a new diorama on the Battle of Palmito Ranch. The diorama was built by students at Highland High School in Gilbert, Arizona, and destined for the Texas Civil War Museum, which funded the project.

The Cameron County Historical Commission is one of 254 county historical commissions in Texas that represents a vital link in the state's preservation efforts. Texas is one of just a few states that have a statewide network of preservation organizations. These commissions have statutory responsibility to initiate and conduct programs suggested by their county commissioners' court and the THC. Over the years, they have worked in a dynamic and positive partnership with the THC to promote local history celebrations and heritage tourism opportunities, as well as other types of preservation projects. By 2012, Bourgeois had asserted himself as a moti-vated and active preservationist, chairing the Cameron County Historical Commission's Civil War Sesquicentennial Committee, leading toward the commemoration of the 150th anniversary of the battle in May 2015. In support of several projects at the site, the commission and the Brownsville Historical Association offered their members' participation in Park Day activities, as well as letters of support for THC grant proposals. The grow-ing pool of stakeholders, both nationally and locally, greatly added to the THC efforts at the battlefield.[23]

Both 2008 and 2009 turned out to be busy and productive years for the THC-led effort to increase interpretation of the Palmito Ranch Battlefield NHL. In 2009, the THC's efforts were featured in the Civil War Trust's *Hallowed Ground* in an article titled "Lone Star Leadership," informing a national audience about the unspoiled character of the land and the criti-cal need to preserve the site. On the eve of the Civil War's sesquicentennial observance, the THC and its growing group of stakeholders were just get-ting started in preserving the site and increasing interpretation at the bat-tlefield in an effort to add another chapter to the nation's understanding of the Civil War.

6

Archeology atop Palmito Hill

In 1999 the staff of the National Park Service's Palo Alto Battlefield National Historic Site produced a report on Palmito Ranch Battlefield, *Battlefield Core Area Identification Report*. An archeological investigation by Charles Haecker, Rolando Garza, and Charles Morris, *An Historical Archeological Perspective of the Battlefield of Palmito Ranch: The Last Conflict of the Great Rebellion*, followed shortly. While immensely helpful to the THC, these reports contained sensitive information that might inadvertently aid relic hunting on the battlefield and were understandably not readily available to the public. The THC identified further research needs for the battlefield and ways to disseminate this information to the general public to promote awareness without jeopardizing the battlefield's integrity. In an effort to identify a potential funding source for this preservation project at Palmito Ranch Battlefield NHL, the THC looked to the National Park Service.[1]

The National Park Service's ABPP promotes the preservation of significant historic battlefields associated with wars on American soil. Thus, the THC began to develop a project that would aid Palmito Ranch Battlefield NHL. The THC could build on data compiled in earlier reports and disseminate the resulting information in a user-friendly format. At the same time, the THC could capitalize on the interest of its growing coalition of local and national stakeholders to further help document the battlefield and aid preservation.

In the spring of 2009, the THC submitted a final application to the ABPP. Through consultation with the ABPP, the National Park Service approved the THC's research design, proposing a noninvasive archeological survey on Palmito Hill in the core battlefield area. The remaining two objectives of the THC's grant consisted of a THC-led public outreach effort to increase awareness of Palmito Ranch Battlefield NHL through four meetings to be held in Brownsville in 2009 and 2010 and the publication of a new heritage tourism brochure to be circulated across the state. Before the end of summer, the Friends of the Texas Historical Commission received word that the ABPP had approved the application and awarded a $20,285 grant for a new project. This marked the second grant awarded to the Military Sites Program in as many years for a project at Palmito Ranch Battlefield NHL.

In fulfillment of one of the ABPP's grant stipulations, THC staff traveled to ABPP headquarters in Washington, DC, and undertook grant manager training in August 2009. After their return to Texas, the THC staff generated a research design for the pending archeological investigation. James Bruseth planned to supervise the basic magnetometer survey for mapping purposes and an additional survey of the three acres with

Site visit to Palmito Hill, December 2009 (courtesy of the Texas Historical Commission).

metal detectors, but he wanted the opportunity to see the terrain prior to the investigation. On December 3, 2009, THC staff joined by historians and battlefield stakeholders conducted a site visit, which allowed historian Jody Ginn the opportunity to lay eyes on the battlefield he had researched through the Ford Papers. Also through walking the landscape, Bruseth was able to visualize the area of investigation for the THC's upcoming archeological investigation.[2]

Successfully executing the archeological investigation research design required the THC staff to understand the battlefield terrain to accurately document the potential importance of Palmito Hill to the outcome of the battle. Palmito Hill is approximately thirty-five feet high at its summit, located on the southern boundary of the battlefield along the Rio Grande. There are no redoubts or forts with palisades made of earthen walls with wood and iron, nor is there a series of reinforced walls that were either defended or breached during the battles. Rather, natural features defined the location of the two battles.

The workshop held in June 2009 provided the THC staff with an introduction to KOCOA, a traditional military analysis applied to battlefield sites as a tool to help establish site boundaries. In an effort to apply this analysis, historians and archeologists look for a defining battlefield feature, which is one that falls within one or more of the five elements of KOCOA. To find an account of defining features, historians often look at after-action reports and other primary sources, such as memoirs, for any descriptions of specific features that might still exist today or for which the archeological evidence can be found.

The Last Conflict was a resource that greatly assisted the THC in understanding the battlefield's landscape. The primary research goal of its authors was to ascertain the approximate western portion of the battlefield. Twice in 2001 and once in 2002, archeologists conducted a sample survey of the battlefield. The project area included a 400-acre tract administered by the US Fish and Wildlife Service and an adjacent 256-acre tract that is privately owned. The areas surveyed included the western approaches to and the area just north of Palmito Hill. A total of 46 acres of the project area were surveyed with metal detectors. This survey resulted in the discovery of nineteen artifacts on US Fish and Wildlife Service property that were attributed to the battle. No artifacts were discovered as a result of sample-surveying the privately held property. According to the authors of *The Last Conflict*, "This could possibly indicate the extreme brevity of the actions on the afternoon of the thirteenth [May], or perhaps that the federal troops had withdrawn from the open field and were utilizing the cover of the dense brush on the low lying hills to the south and east of the open prairie [Palmito Hill]."[3]

The authors also took into consideration the earlier September 1864 Battle of Palmito Ranch and the potential existence of earlier artifacts dating to that multiday battle. Haecker, Garza, and Morris noted, "On September 6, 1864, Federal Infantry, supported by a force of Mexican Nationalists, attacked the Confederate cavalry outpost at Palmito Ranch. A Confederate cavalry counterattack, led by Colonel William [*sic*] Carrington, recaptured the San Martin and Palmito Ranch positions on September 9. Several follow-up skirmishes occurred in the vicinity of Palmito Ranch until September 12, when the Federal troops retreated to their base at Brazos Santiago."

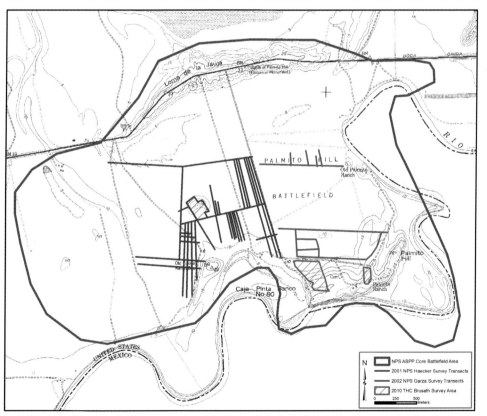

Palmito Ranch Battlefield, surveyed areas of core battlefield area (courtesy of Rolando Garza, Palo Alto Battlefield National Historical Park, National Park Service).

To their credit, the authors hypothesized that the artifact pattern detected during their surveys of the core area of the battlefield could be a result of the September 1864 battle. However, their investigation ultimately concluded that "documentary evidence suggests this artifact patterning resulted from a relatively minor engagement that occurred on the afternoon of May 13, 1865."[4]

According to *The Last Conflict*, there are "four, seemingly immutable topographic features from which historians demarcate the battlefield: the Rio Grande, Palmito Hill, Tulosa Hill and Loma de Juaja."[5] In their work, Haecker, Garza, and Morris produced a report that included an archeological survey within the core battlefield area of Palmito Ranch Battlefield NHL but not atop Palmito Hill. Because the CWT owned property on top of that defining battlefield feature and because the THC had obtained ABPP funding, the THC had an obvious opportunity to add significantly to the documentation of the national historic landmark.[6]

THC staff then looked to the historical record for verification that Palmito Hill was in fact mentioned in the accounts of Union or Confederate forces during either of the battles. The site's National Historic Landmark file, secondary sources, and Ginn's research in the Ford Papers soon began to paint a picture of Palmito Hill's limited but real role in the Battle of Palmito Ranch.

During the Civil War, visual contact was necessary to strike at the enemy. The reason that Palmito Ranch was chosen as a semipermanent outpost for the Confederates, and later became the site of two battles between Union and Confederate forces, was that the surrounding terrain was well suited to the traditional Euro-American military tactics of the time. A substantial number of records found in the Ford Papers, including after-action reports by several commanders who participated in the first battle and numerous standard field reports and returns submitted by other commanders stationed at the site throughout late 1864 and early 1865, clearly indicated that Palmito Ranch became a strategically significant outpost. Its position, approximately halfway between Fort Brown and Brazos Santiago Depot, made it a convenient spot for Confederate detachments to send pickets to observe the activities of the Union army and quickly report back. As a result, it became a strategically significant outpost for the Confederate defense of Fort Brown, Brownsville, and the intermittent and erratic (but frequently lucrative and therefore valuable) cross-border cotton trade.[7]

The Ford Papers indicate that while none of the Confederate commanders at Palmito Ranch provided a detailed analysis of the terrain surrounding the site, their notes on activities document the advantages provided by elements such as hills, chaparral, sand hills, and ravines. The commanders recognized and regularly exploited such features to their military advantage, both in active combat and in routine defensive and surveillance activities. To gain a better understanding of what lay before them (i.e., Confederate troop movements and defensive strong points), on May 12–13, 1865, Union officers occupied the available high ground at Palmito Hill to gain a vantage point for their own observations and a tactical advantage. The slightly elevated position allowed the Federal infantry—who did not have the benefit of artillery or cavalry during the 1865 battle—to observe their fast-moving mounted opponents as they approached through the chaparral and to conceal their movements in response to the Confederate advance.

Unfortunately, the US War Department did not produce a map of either the September 1864 or May 1865 engagements at Palmito Ranch. Nevertheless, accredited historic secondary sources such as Jeff William Hunt's *The Last Battle of the Civil War: Palmetto Ranch*; primary documents such as the Ford Papers; and official reports such as the 1997 National Historic Landmark nomination, the 1999 battlefield study, and *The Last Conflict* have all helped establish a much clearer understanding of the troop movements on May 12–13, 1865, and thus greatly aided the KOCOA analysis.

The following three excerpts, from *The Last Battle, The War of the Rebellion*, and the 1997 Palmito Ranch Battlefield NHL nomination, all indicate a Union presence near the base of and atop Palmito Hill at various points in the battle on May 13, 1865.

> The units picked for the movement to the hill were Company K, under the command of Second Lieutenant Charles A. Jones, and Company A, Captain Stillman C. Montgomery commanding, of the 34th Indiana....The Rebel cavalry were ... putting up a fight ... and firing continued as the men from the 34th Indiana pushed the Southerners back toward Palmetto Hill. . . . Lieutenant Jones soon reached the banks of the Rio Grande to the left [facing south] of the bluff. [Losing sight of his fellow unit, Company A (somewhere to his right), Jones decided to lead his men to the top of Palmito Hill so that] he could see what was going on. . . . Shortly afterward, Captain William C. Durkee of the 62nd United States Colored Troops and assistant

acting inspector general at Brazos Santiago, came riding up to Jones'
command. [With no new orders from Colonel Barrett,] Jones ordered his company down from the crest of Palmetto Hill. . . . Here
his men were within easy range of the Confederates and the firing
became very heavy. Company K seemed to be badly exposed.[8]

[May 12, 1865] I immediately started for Palmetto Ranch [from White's
Ranch], skirmishing most of the way with the enemy's cavalry, and drove
them, at noon, from their camp, which had been occupied by about 190
men and horses, capturing 3 prisoners, 2 horses, and 4 beef-cattle, and
their ten days' rations, just issued. Halted on the hill at Palmetto Ranch
to rest and feed men and animals. While there at 3 p.m. a considerable
force of the enemy appeared, and the position being indefensible, I fell
back to White's Ranch for the night, skirmishing some of the way, and
had one man of the Second Texas Cavalry wounded. . . .

In this [May 13, 1865] engagement our forces [Colonel Theodore H.
Barrett, 62nd US Colored Infantry] charged the enemy [Confederate],
compelling him to abandon his cover, and pursuing him, drove him
across an open prairie. . . . The enemy having been driven several miles
since daylight, and our men needing rest, it was not deemed prudent

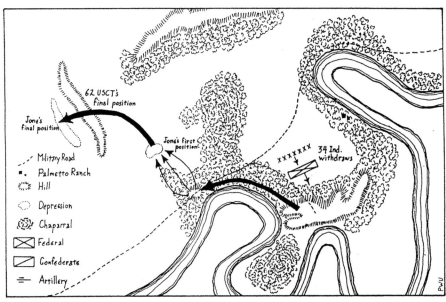

The Federal attack, Battle of Palmito Ranch (from Hunt, *The Last Battle of the Civil
War*, 78).

to advance farther. Therefore, relinquishing the pursuit, we returned to a hill about a mile from Palmetto Ranch, where the 34th Indiana had already taken its position.[9]

After the brief skirmishing [against members of Gidding's Regiment (Confederate States of America) on May 12] at Palmito Ranch, [Lt. Colonel David] Branson and his Union troops retreated to the hill nearby to rest and feed their animals. At approximately 3 p.m., however, the Confederates appeared with reinforcements. Branson considered the Federal's position *on* Palmito Hill to be "indefensible," so he led his troops back to White's Ranch for the night.[10]

As the historical written record indicates, Union forces in fact did use Palmito Hill in the 1865 battle. Supported by the principles of KOCOA military analysis, Palmito Hill does provide an elevated point from which Union observation of Confederate troops on the afternoon of May 13, 1865, was possible. It does offer an avenue of approach for a Union flanking maneuver of Confederate troops who were attempting to delay the Union advance northwest of Palmito Hill. In sum, this historical evidence helped shape the THC's approach toward its ABPP grant objective to examine a portion of Palmito Hill through an archeological investigation for evidence that the hill served as both an observation point and an avenue of approach for the Union forces during the battle. Successful completion of this objective would then allow the THC to prepare information for the public about historic preservation of the battlefield. It also would have a secondary benefit of allowing the THC to more thoroughly evaluate the CWT's three acres of Palmito Hill for acceptance into state trusteeship through the THC's Leave a Legacy/Land Banking Program.[11]

The THC's research design called for a basic magnetometer survey for mapping purposes and an additional survey with metal detectors, but to accomplish this, the THC needed support at the battlefield. The National Park Service's informal "good-neighbor policy," whereby staff at a nearby national park will aid, whenever possible, in any activities associated with the preservation of an existing National Historic Landmark, greatly benefited the THC's project. Palo Alto Battlefield National Historic Site archeologist/chief of resource management Rolando Garza, historian Douglas Murphy, and newly arrived park superintendent Mark Spier all assisted in varying capacities with the archeological investigations in 2010. Proper examination of the historical record of the Rio Grande's shifting channel prior to the project assisted THC staff and the volunteer archeologists—led by Garza—with the 2010 survey on Palmito Hill by confirming that the THC-surveyed tracts lay north of the Rio Grande prior to the Civil War.[12]

As one of the major owners of the land surrounding the CWT's three acres, the US Fish and Wildlife Service provided key services during the March 9–11, 2010, survey. Refuge manager Bryan Winton and his staff are the stewards of approximately 776 plant species found within the vast boundaries of the South Texas Refuge Complex. This includes thorny brush as the predominant native vegetation type and the palmetto tree, for which the historic ranch and battlefield were named. In consideration of the vegetation and abundant fauna, such as the reclusive ocelot found in the LRGV Refuge, the US Fish and Wildlife Service mowed the survey area, carefully clearing vegetation that would hinder the movement of the THC's magnetometer cart and metal detectors. Throughout the multiday survey, the refuge staff observed the historians and archeologists' efforts to protect the habitat of species located on Palmito Hill. The result was a completed survey with no lasting harm imposed on the environment.

Pursuant to Bruseth's research design, the magnetometer survey began in the cleared strips provided by the US Fish and Wildlife Service by pulling a cart with two magnetometer sensors on a grid across the strips. Bill Pierson, a THC archeologist and remote-sensing specialist, assisted in setting up a base station unit near the survey area to collect large-scale diurnal magnetic data for later correction with the cart data. The data were stored during the day in the magnetometer consoles and downloaded to a laptop computer from which magnetic maps, showing the distribution of ferrous metal, were produced each evening. Ultimately, the THC produced a final map of the field magnetic survey.

Following the magnetometer survey, under the supervision of Garza and Bruseth, local volunteers used metal detectors to relocate each ferrous magnetic anomaly and excavated artifacts to see if they were from the battle period. Nonferrous items encountered were also excavated to see if they represented the battle period. From the outset, only battle-period artifacts were planned for collection and curation.

On the second day of the investigation, local landowner and then professor of anthropology at the University of Texas at Brownsville, Antonio N. Zavaleta, stopped by to observe the investigation. A longtime enthusiast of the battle's history, Zavaleta invited THC staff to his neighboring prop-

THC remote-sensing specialist Bill Pierson conducts a magnetometer survey of mowed portions of CWT's three acres atop Palmito Hill, March 2010 (courtesy of Texas Historical Commission).

erty on top of Palmito Hill. There they were served a meal that Zavaleta described as a "ranch-style lunch." While on his property, Zavaleta provided the THC and US Fish and Wildlife Service staff with a walking tour of his family's agricultural pasture, which covered a portion of Palmito Hill's western edge. Before the day was over, the THC had an invitation to survey an additional twenty acres of Palmito Hill. The opportunity to survey the Zavaleta tract, through a second research methodology drafted by Bruseth, demonstrates the core ingredient that has helped save Palmito Ranch Battlefield NHL, stressed throughout this book. Whether local or national, a growing coalition of stakeholders has lent their special talents and resources to the historic preservation of the battlefield. In October

2010, THC staff returned to the site for a second archeological investigation focused on the Zavaleta tract, continuing their effort to locate evidence of Union or Confederate forces atop Palmito Hill.

During the March 2010 investigation, the THC staffers and their associates encountered significant obstructions outside the mowed transects because of the dense vegetation. However, the availability of the nearby twenty-acre Zavaleta tract to the west did not have such an abundance of this natural obstacle. The survey methodology for investigating the Zavaleta tract consisted of east-to-west transects to conform to the plowed furrows of the agricultural field. A line of seven volunteers who were experienced metal-detector operators, again led by Garza, lined up along the western boundary of the survey area at roughly two- to three-meter intervals starting at the northwest corner of the survey area. The survey crew proceeded to transect due east while maintaining their spacing, with some having to lag behind to avoid interference from machines working on the same frequency. The crew used overlapping swings of the metal-detector coil to

THC archeologists and historians, staff from the National Park Service's Palo Alto Battlefield National Historical Park, and volunteers conduct a metal-detector survey of the Zavaleta Tract of Palmito Hill, October 2010 (courtesy of Texas Historical Commission).

ensure adequate coverage of the area. Wooden survey stakes with colored flagging tape were used to keep the survey transects in line from one end of the survey area to the other. When the survey crew arrived at the eastern boundary of the survey area, they shifted the line to the south and transect-ed west, coming back across the southern stakes of the previous transect, until they reached the western boundary of the survey area. This process was repeated until the northern half of the survey area had been systematically covered. All metal signals or anomalies were investigated by the operators during the transect.

After completing a systematic survey of the northern half of the Zavale-ta tract and finding no battlefield-related artifacts, Bruseth made a change in methodology for the remainder of the investigation. This effort covered about 60 percent of the southern half, and the survey became more of a reconnaissance. The strategy was to examine this portion of the tract as thoroughly as possible given the vegetation and terrain limitations to see if any battlefield-related artifacts were present.

Recording field data from a metal-detector survey of the Zavaleta tract of Palmito Hill, October 2010. Left to right: Toni Turner, archeologist and volunteer; Rolando Garza, chief of resource management, Palo Alto Battlefield National Historical Park; and Jim Bruseth, chief archeologist, THC (courtesy of the Texas Historical Commission).

Bruseth, Garza, and Toni Turner followed behind the metal-detector operators, bagging and assigning a Shovel Test (ST) number to the artifacts, which were collected and placed in a plastic bag with the ST number and other pertinent information displayed on the bag. All clearly non-battlefield-related or modern material was left in place.

Seven artifacts were collected during the March 2010 survey of the CWT's three acres. Subsequent analysis and identification by the THC and the NPS eliminated all as being battlefield related. Two artifacts were collected during the October 2010 survey of the Zavaleta tract. Neither could be associated with either the first or second battles at Palmito Ranch.

Ultimately, the THC's investigations atop Palmito Hill were unable to confirm, through the recovery of Civil War-era battlefield artifacts, that the promontory served as a point for observation or for an avenue of approach by Union forces during the May 13, 1865, battle. Nevertheless, the THC's 2010 archeological investigations, and the preparations undertaken in 2009, had the positive outcome of building a strong esprit de corps between the THC, the US Fish and Wildlife Service, the National Park Service, the Cameron County Historical Commission, the Brownsville Historical Association, and other local stakeholders on the eve of the Civil War's sesquicentennial.[13]

The archeological investigation was the primary objective of the THC's 2009 ABPP grant, but it was not the only one. The other objectives were a series of public meetings and a brochure that offered the THC an opportunity to promote heritage tourism to the battlefield and raise awareness of the site. In an effort to engage a larger, more diverse audience and promote the unique international Civil War history of the Palmito Ranch Battlefield NHL, the THC began facilitating public meetings in the fall of 2009. Held in Cameron County, the meetings were designed to engage the local community with the battlefield and its history and hopefully in its preservation for future generations.

The first of four public meetings took place in 2009 at the Brownsville Historical Association's Market Square in downtown Brownsville. Historic in its own right, the Market Square location provided the perfect setting for the meeting's attendees to embrace the rich historical fabric of Brownsville. The second meeting was held in April 2010 at Palo Alto Battlefield National Historical Park's visitor center in conjunction with that year's Park Day. This location not only provided the opportunity for a local stakeholder to host a public meeting; it also allowed attendees to better familiarize themselves with the National Park Sevice's role in the Rio Grande Valley. The third meeting was also held at Palo Alto Battlefield NHP in September 2010 as part of the site's yearly Rio Grande Delta Archeology Fair. The final public outreach meeting was again held with the Brownsville Historical Association in December 2010. The meeting served as a roll-out venue for the THC's third ABPP grant objective, a new full-color brochure detailing the project. The production of twenty thousand copies of this heritage travel brochure provided the THC with a handsome handout. It informed the public of the existence of the last land battle of the Civil War and served to increase regional awareness of the need for preservation and enhancement of the site as the sesquicentennial observance approached in May 2015.

The THC's effort at Palmito Ranch Battlefield NHL could not have succeeded without the combined support of both local and national stakeholders. Although the THC project's primary objective did not produce definitive evidence of a Civil War–era presence on top of Palmito Hill, the combined efforts during the projects ultimately aided the preservation of the National Historic Landmark battlefield.

7

Getting the Word Out

AM Radio and Workshops

With the completion of the two Palmito Hill archeological investigations in 2010, the THC Military Sites Program had worked on projects associated with the battlefield for three years.

In March 2010, while driving along the roads that border and lead into Palmito Ranch Battlefield NHL in an effort to carry out the KOCOA analysis, THC staff realized that the battlefield needed an on-site presence to direct heritage tourists. But how to accomplish this? In 2010 there were no funds at the THC to pay for staffing the site. The local stakeholders, while available for limited projects on-site, had their own jobs that required their attention and thus could not staff the battlefield on a daily basis. The solution was that the battlefield needed a presence that never slept, could work day after day, rain or shine. The THC met the need through technology, continued partnerships with stakeholders, and multiple foundations' willingness to invest in the heritage tourism benefit to the public.

A site that maintains its historic integrity yet has no on-site representation or interpretation provides heritage tourists with little information concerning its significance. The THC developed a project for installing a continuous radio broadcast system and accompanying signage that could provide visitors driving the length of the Palmito Ranch Battlefield NHL with the historical narrative of the battles. Called Exploring the Boundaries:

Palmito Ranch Battlefield National Historic Landmark project, the battlefield was about to receive its most modern interpretive effort.

The THC and the Friends of the Texas Historical Commission sought and received funding for the project in 2010 from the National Park Service's Heritage Partnership Program, with supplementing funding requests from two private donors—the Texas Historical Foundation and the Society of the Order of the Southern Cross. The THC and the Friends of the Texas Historical Commission looked to a first-time funding source to raise the final funding necessary to complete the radio broadcast repeater and signage project. The US Fish and Wildlife Service administered a Challenge Cost Share Grant program to support partnerships not only for the restoration, protection, enhancement, and management of important fish and wildlife habitats on its own or private lands but also for the enhancement of education projects.[1]

The Battle of Palmito Ranch retains excellent integrity and conveys a powerful impact through its setting. This is not due to luck or simply the site's remoteness, literally at the bottom of the state of Texas. The NHL retains such outstanding integrity due to the conscientious land management practices of private landowners and the exceptional natural conservation efforts of the US Fish and Wildlife Service's South Texas Refuge Complex.[2]

In March 2011 the US Fish and Wildlife Service was again there for the THC's latest interpretive project at the battlefield, from start to finish. In 2010, they had been on-site during the archeological investigation on Palmito Hill. When it was time to install the radio broadcast repeater antenna on March 24, 2011, the US Fish and Wildlife Service was on-site again to monitor the flora and fauna and provide electricians to help install the unit and bring power to the site. Information Station Specialists (ISS), the radio broadcast repeater system provider, worked diligently to install and calibrate the system that day. Afterward, the ISS traveled to the National Park Service's headquarters building in Brownsville, where the staff provided the THC with a hands-on training session for the radio broadcast repeater system, the most important aspect of which was how to record a message and upload it into the system's USB interface. The THC greatly appreciated the "good-neighbor" support from the Palo Alto Battlefield National Historical Park staff.

The funds raised and the system installed, the THC worked to finish a narrative for the radio broadcast, as well as the final layout of the accompanying signage. With both pieces of interpretation, the THC wanted to

Installation of the radio broadcast repeater system, March 24, 2011 (courtesy of the Texas Historical Commission).

be as descriptive as possible to be helpful to battlefield visitors. Primary-document research of the Ford Papers, combined with the National Historic Landmark narrative, secondary sources, archeological reports, and other sources, was used to help craft the broadcast.

In less than one month, THC staff returned to the battlefield to complete the broadcast repeater project. On April 25, they returned with new Texas Department of Transportation (TxDOT) advanced general information signage and a full-color wayside panel for heritage tourists visiting the battlefield. That morning, THC staff met with staff from the local office of TxDOT and the US Fish and Wildlife Service, who arrived with heavy equipment to dig the necessary holes—while safeguarding the local habitat—to place the new signage under the guidance of TxDOT. While on-site, the THC accessed the radio broadcast repeater system and installed the new historical narrative message.

The dedication ceremony for the new radio broadcast repeater and its accompanying signage formed the centerpiece for the fourth Park Day at Palmito Ranch Battlefield NHL on May 10, 2011. Joining the general public were representatives from the local and national stakeholders the THC had

Dedication of the radio broadcast repeater system and signage, May 10, 2011 (courtesy of the Texas Historical Commission).

cultivated over the past three and half years, including the Brownsville Historical Association, US Fish and Wildlife Service, Cameron County Historical Commission, and National Park Service's Palo Alto Battlefield National Historical Park, as well as an adjacent landowner. Each of these partners and the special people who represented them had given their time, energy, and passion toward saving Palmito Ranch Battlefield NHL, and the THC owed them a great debt of gratitude.

During the early part of the sesquicentennial of the Civil War, the THC's objective of continuing efforts to enhance interpretation and preservation of Palmito Ranch Battlefield NHL focused on two primary goals: greatly improving the limited interpretation on-site (a lone Texas Historic Marker) and launching a major effort to further educate visitors, specifically an interpretive viewing platform in the core battlefield area. With the radio broadcast repeater and the new interpretive signage dedicated in May 2011, the THC had addressed the previous lack of interpretation on-site.

The broadcast repeater, transmitting on 1610 AM, has been successful in helping get the word out about the battlefield. However, by Federal Communications Commission regulation, the repeater can broadcast only locally within a radius of about ten miles. How could the THC get the word out even farther during the sesquicentennial? In August 2010, the THC applied for a new grant from the SOSC to provide the agency's Military Sites Program with even more capacity to promote the rich history of Palmito Ranch Battlefield NHL during the sesquicentennial. The application requested funding to conduct triannual, regional Sesquicentennial Outreach Workshops focusing on the THC's preservation efforts at Palmito Ranch Battlefield and to showcase agency assets that tell the story of Texas' involvement in the Civil War (i.e., state historic sites, Marker Program, historic cemetery, National Register files, and website). In addition, the workshops were designed to provide the local co-host with the opportunity to showcase its efforts to preserve local Civil War history and to invite a local historian to lecture on an aspect of the community's Civil War history.[3]

On April 27, 2011, the THC conducted the first Sesquicentennial Outreach Workshop at the Austin History Center. After a presentation on the THC's efforts at Palmito Ranch Battlefield NHL since 2007, Austin History Center staff used the venue as an opening for a new temporary exhibit on the topic of secession and its impact on Austin in 1861. After this successful workshop, on August 25, the Webb County Heritage Foundation in Laredo co-hosted the series' second workshop, providing attendees with

Sesquicentennial Outreach Workshop, Laredo, August 25, 2011 (courtesy of the Texas Historical Commission).

Sesquicentennial Outreach Workshop, Galveston, November 3, 2012 (courtesy of the Texas Historical Commission).

a presentation from local historians about the 1863 Battle of Laredo and opening a new temporary exhibit, "Texas Border during the Civil War." The following spring, on March 17, 2012, the THC brought the workshop series to Tyler, where the Smith County Historical Society served as co-host and provided lectures on its community's efforts to preserve the site of Camp Ford, a prisoner-of-war camp for Union troops during the war.

A second grant from the SOSC in 2011, the fourth grant to the THC to date for projects undertaken for Palmito Ranch Battlefield NHL, made possible two additional workshops in this series. On August 2, 2012, THC staff traveled to Cross Plains to join the Callahan County Historical Commission. Later that year on November 3 the THC met with the Galveston Historical Foundation, joined by the Galveston County Historical Commission. Two of the co-host organizations found the THC workshops to be excellent opportunities to promote their own local historic preservation projects. The Callahan County Historical Commission provided attendees with a lecture on its efforts to interpret the history of the Texas frontier during the Civil War. The Galveston Historical Foundation used the opportunity to promote upcoming programs associated with the 150th anniversary of the Battle of Galveston on January 1, 2013, and the sesquicentennial observance of Juneteenth in 2015. Through the five workshops, more and more people were learning about Texas Civil War history and the THC's preservation efforts at Palmito Ranch Battlefield NHL.

By 2012, the THC's Military Sites Program increased its capacity to enhance the research, interpretation, and preservation efforts associated with Palmito Ranch Battlefield NHL and, equally as important, got the word out to Texans about this important historic site. Although this battle was small in scale when compared to the epic confrontations back east during the Civil War, the fact is that the war finally ended in a field in Texas, not at Appomattox Court House, which is significant. This on-site interpretation shares with battlefield visitors a much greater understanding of the 1865 battle's multicultural and international implications due to its proximity to Mexico (the South's only international border during the war). This significance has helped generate support for preserving the unspoiled character of the site and ultimately helps save Palmito Ranch Battlefield.

8

On the Eve of the Sesquicentennial

The THC staff's November 2007 visit to the three acres atop Palmito Hill owned by the CWT set in motion an eight-year effort that produced a coalition of partners in preservation. The visit was also the beginning of what would lead to a number of projects that culminated in increased interpretation and raised awareness, which helped save the battlefield from neglect and obscurity. On the eve of the sesquicentennial of the Battle of Palmito Ranch the THC continued to work on new projects, such as this book, new on-site interpretation, and the possibility of accepting a portion of the battlefield from the CWT.

The mission of the THC is to protect and preserve the state's historic and prehistoric resources for the use, education, enjoyment, and economic benefit of present and future generations. Shortly before THC staff undertook their first site visit to Palmito Ranch Battlefield NHL in the fall of 2007, the THC took over the administration of eighteen state historic sites from its sister state agency, the Texas Parks and Wildlife Department. From whitewashed ruins and Victorian mansions to sacred burial mounds and pivotal battlegrounds, such as the Sabine Pass Battleground State Historic Site, the THC's historic sites exemplify the extent of Texas history. This addition to the THC's two existing state historic sites, the National Museum of the Pacific War in Fredericksburg and the Sam Rayburn House Museum in Bonham, meant that the THC was in just a short time managing twenty diverse cultural sites across the Lone Star State; however, none of these were located in the Rio Grande Valley.[1]

With the transfer of the eighteen historic sites, the Texas legislature also provided the THC with the authority to accept additional properties as state historic sites. Beginning almost immediately, THC staff in consultation with the CWT discussed the possibility of a land donation. If funding for interpretive efforts could be acquired, the addition of Palmito Ranch Battlefield to the THC's newly formed State Historic Sites Division would most certainly provide heritage tourists with visitor service programs and wayside exhibits that tell the story of the last military engagement of the Civil War. It would also aid in highlighting a portion of the state's rich cultural heritage at a time when interest in the Civil War would be growing during the sesquicentennial of the war (2011–2015). Such an acquisition would also give the THC a state historic site in the Rio Grande Valley. Opportunity, yes, but the fact remained that the THC headquarters in Austin is more than a five-hour drive from the battlefield, and in 2008 the THC was busily undertaking the successful management of eighteen new state historic sites along with its two existing sites. As a result, acceptance of the CWT's property at Palmito Ranch Battlefield NHL into the THC's new State Historic Sites Division did not materialize.

In 2009, THC staff met with the newly appointed THC executive director, Mark Wolfe, regarding the CWT's standing offer for the three-acre tract. From this meeting, the THC sent the CWT a letter indicating that the agency was willing to evaluate the property through the THC's Leave a Legacy/Land Banking Program, administered through the agency's Archeology Division. The CWT agreed to the request and granted THC staff permission to conduct an archeological investigation of its tract in March 2010.

Unfortunately, the THC's future was uncertain in early 2011 due to possible significant cuts to the agency's budget by the legislature. Many THC projects not already funded and under way were tabled until the end of the fiscal year, when the upcoming biennium's budget was signed into law. Naturally, this included further examination into accepting the CWT's donation. CWT leaders, to their credit, understood the agency's position, staying in tacit communication throughout 2011 and encouragingly inquiring for updates.[2]

In the spring of 2012, the THC and the CWT again began correspondence regarding the three-acre tract. A new director for the THC's Archeology Division, Pat Mercado-Allinger, took over following the retirement of former division director James Bruseth. With the recent uncertainty of the past legislative session behind them, and the support of Mercado-Allinger for proceeding with an analysis of the proposed donation, the THC was again ready to take up the consideration of accepting the donation. That summer THC historians and archeologists worked on vetting the donation. This process required the evaluation of the property by staff. Their report was then presented to agency commissioners at two quarterly meetings. Initially, presentation of the staff's assessment was scheduled for the agency's July 2012 quarterly meeting, but a full docket of items pushed the item to October of that year.

At the THC's October 25, 2012, quarterly meeting staff provided their findings from the March 2010 archeological survey and the subsequent internal evaluation assessment in the THC's Short-Form Program Proposal. Staff's recommendation, that the THC accept the proposed donation of land as is with no foreseeable plans to develop the site, thus focused on preserving its natural and historic integrity. The THC commissioners left the meeting in agreement that the staff return in January 2013 with a Long-Form Program Proposal.

At the January 24, 2013, quarterly meeting, THC staff presented a final assessment of the site that called for acceptance of the donation, including deed work. Afterward staff would draft a State Archeological Landmark nomination for the site, followed by the development of a written management plan. THC commissioners voted to accept the property, but prior to moving forward on deed work, they asked the staff to contact the CWT regarding existing language on access in their property's deed, including the CWT's willingness to pay for a new survey of the tract. The last property survey associated with the CWT land on Palmito Hill was undertaken in 2001 when the CWT originally purchased the property. Thanks to the CWT, in September 2013 a new boundary survey was completed, and THC staff provided an update at the agency's October 2013 quarterly meeting. At the January 2014 quarterly meeting, THC commissioners voted to accept the donation as one parcel of 3.07 acres. Throughout these meetings, the CWT worked on their end to clarify the access language in their deed. At the time of this book's publication THC staff were still working with the CWT to finalize the access language with neighboring landowners, paving the way for the THC to finally accept the CWT parcel. Should the THC be able to receive the tract atop Palmito Hill, it will likely become a part of the THC's Land Banking holdings with no plans for future development, thus preserving the integrity of the battlefield.[3]

On the eve of the battle's sesquicentennial, the THC's Military Sites Program had already accomplished much toward saving Palmito Ranch Battlefield NHL thanks to the assistance of local and national stakeholders and the support of many generous donors. In total, the THC completed two archeological investigations, published a heritage tourism brochure, hosted four public meetings around Brownsville to raise public awareness, installed a radio broadcast repeater and new onsite signage, and conducted five regional outreach workshops across the state. And the THC has continued to co-host Park Days at the battlefield each year since 2008.

While it had been present from the beginning as a local stakeholder, the Cameron County Historical Commission (CCHC), with its ambitious sesquicentennial commemoration planning, asserted itself by 2013 into a leading role in co-hosting Park Day at Palmito Ranch Battlefield NHL. On April 13, 2013, Wilson Bourgeois, chair of the CCHC's Civil War Sesquicentennial Committee, and his fellow committee members hosted a well-attended morning symposium at the historic Cameron County Courthouse in downtown Brownsville. That year, the symposium served as the morning session for Park Day activities held later that day at the battlefield. The event was in its sixth year at Palmito Ranch Battlefield NHL, and in an effort to keep it fresh, the CCHC placed its signature on Park Day by adding

Park Day 2013 (courtesy of the Texas Historical Commission).

additional academic discussion on Civil War historical topics to the already established discussion about the Battle of Palmito Ranch. The symposium was headlined by keynote speaker Charles Graff, a native of Brownsville and adjunct professor of history at the then University of Texas at Brownsville, who provided the attendees with a presentation on "Religion in the Civil War." As an official State of Texas representative to the CWT for Park Day activities at the battlefield, William McWhorter provided attendees with a historical account of the Battle of Palmito Ranch and the preservation efforts undertaken by the THC and its partners at the national historic landmark over the past five years.[4]

On April 13, US Fish and Wildlife Service refuge managers Jennifer Owen-White and Bryan Winton, along with staff from the South Texas Refuge Complex, co-hosted the afternoon session of Park Day. At the battlefield, US Fish and Wildlife Service staff provided an orientation on the South Texas Refuge Complex's mission as well as hands-on natural resources conservation activities. Joining the effort that day, Palo Alto Battlefield National Historical Park staff attended and distributed the National Park Service's

Cameron County Historical Commission Civil War symposium, November 2, 2013 (courtesy of the Texas Historical Commission).

newly published Civil War trading cards that featured figures from the Civil War in South Texas. Park Day 2013 concluded with an informal session on the upcoming 2015 sesquicentennial and in microcosm illustrated the successful THC-led effort for the battlefield. Each stakeholder brought examples of what its organization "does for a living" and thus enhanced the visitors' experiences at Palmito Ranch Battlefield NHL, helping to engage a wider audience in the battlefield's story.[5]

The CCHC's symposium that 2013 spring day led to its hosting another symposium later that year on November 2. Attendees were presented with a call to attend the following year's Park Day, welcoming even more local volunteers to the growing number interested in preserving Palmito Ranch Battlefield. With their two symposiums that year drawing crowds, speaking with confidence about the history of the battle, and asserting itself as the local driving force working to observe the upcoming sesquicentennial in 2015, the CCHC demonstrated how a local volunteer effort with the assistance of state and national stakeholders could contribute greatly to saving Palmito Ranch Battlefield.

At Park Day on April 4, 2014, the morning's session was once again coordinated by the CCHC's Civil War Sesquicentennial Committee. This time the academic historical symposium was held at Palo Alto Battlefield National Historical Park. In seeking out cooperation with its local partner in preservation, the CCHC worked to keep its venues fresh for Rio Grande Valley history lovers. The symposium's keynote speaker was historian Jim Mills, who discussed the topic "South Texas and the Cotton Trade in the Civil War." The outstanding organization and promotion efforts of the committee resulted in the largest crowd for a Park Day in Texas to date, with 185 people attending.[6]

As its planning was yet to be finalized by this point, the CCHC was somewhat tight-lipped about its plans for commemorating the battle's sesquicentennial. Still, the members encouraged attendees in April 2014 to stay in touch with the commission's website and Facebook page for further word on how the nation's last military commemoration of the sesquicentennial would play out in their community of Brownsville.

The CCHC was not the only battlefield stakeholder with a surprise to share with attendees at Park Day 2014. Standing on historic ground or in a historic structure puts people in the perfect frame of mind to consider their cultural heritage, gaining a "sense of place" and the importance of preserving it for future generations. As previously noted, after having reviewed documents in the THC's files dating back to 2001, it was clear to McWhorter that the US Fish and Wildlife Service, the National Park Service, and other parties had been interested for years in constructing a viewing platform somewhere within the boundaries of the National Historic Landmark. As early as May 2008, the THC had met with the CCHC, US Fish and Wildlife Service, and local National Park Service staff to discuss long-range projects at the battlefield. Included was the possibility of a viewing platform in the core battlefield area. But where would (or more important, should) such a platform be placed? And who would pay for it?

The location of the viewing platform was decided by, and built through the generosity of, the South Texas Refuge Complex. At Park Day in April

US Fish and Wildlife Service viewing platform, Palmito Ranch Battlefield's core battlefield area, 2014 (courtesy of the Texas Historical Commission).

2014, Refuge Manager Winton unveiled the new viewing platform located on the agency's land within the core battlefield. The viewing platform accomplished the local stakeholders' goal of enhancing interpretation from a lone historical marker to include a first-class venue where visitors can learn more about the battlefield, in time for the battlefield's sesquicentennial commemoration.

According to the THC's report *Economic Impact of Historic Preservation in Texas*, updated in 2015,

> Historic sites and cultural heritage are crucial drivers of travel activity in Texas and across the nation. Business and leisure travelers to Texas who cited "visit a historic site" as a primary activity directly spent close to $7.3 billion in 2013, accounting for approximately 12.5 percent of total direct travel spending in Texas. These expenditures support hotels, motels, bed and breakfasts, food establishments, and other local retail and service businesses. Although the Alamo is the most visited heritage tourism site in Texas, heritage travelers visit all the regions of the state and on average spend more in their travels than the typical visitor. Heritage tourists seek out not only historic sites open to the public, but also the cultural heritage that fills every small town and major city.[7]

How timely was it that also in May 2014 a planning meeting was held that led to the creation of the Rio Grande Valley Civil War Trail? The trail launched in February 2015, marking dozens of sites, including Palmito Ranch Battlefield, on a trail guide and website that includes podcasts in English and Spanish. With this new heritage tourism effort, Palmito Ranch Battlefield gained yet another local stakeholder, and representatives from the Rio Grande Valley Civil War Trail participated a few months later in observation of the sesquicentennial of the battlefield.[8]

Through this observance the CCHC's Civil War Sesquicentennial Committee wanted to encourage the community to remember its role in the Civil War. Leading up to the May 2015 commemoration, the committee found that

> the key to the sesquicentennial is not to reflect on the battles or causes of the war for those items are long since gone, but of the memory of the men. From the generals like Lee or Grant down to the lowest privates, like . . . John Jefferson Williams [the last soldier killed in the Civ-

il War], all of these men gave to their causes and sacrificed for them. The sacrifices that helped make the land known as the "The Free and the Brave," the land of these United States.[9]

The week of May 11–16, 2015, was billed by the committee as "one for the history books." To their credit, the CCHC's Civil War Sesquicentennial Committee worked diligently toward a weeklong series of events; however, they were not able to deliver their grand commemoration due to unexpected complications in the planning process and a loss of key personnel in the committee a few months earlier. By March 2015, the commission decided it was necessary to cancel all plans but the actual 150th anniversary commemoration.[10]

On Tuesday, May 12, the committee led a commemorative ceremony at the battlefield at the interpretive viewing platform. That day, heavy rains and lightning forced yet another last-minute change in the planned ceremony. About sixty people joined the CCHC chair, Steve Hathcock, for a brief speech and an artillery salute provided by Civil War–era reenactors Knibb's Battery, Artillery Regiment, 1st Division, Army of Northern Virginia, commanded by Capt. Jim Cochrane of Richmond, Virginia. Two hours later the remainder of the sesquicentennial ceremony was held indoors at the Brownsville Historical Association, where Craig Stone and commission members were joined by speakers and the public for a brief ceremony that honored the history of the battle. With this ceremony the battle's sesquicentennial anniversary observance concluded, but not the THC or its stakeholders' efforts at Palmito Ranch Battlefield NHL.

Epilogue

The original 2010 report on the Ford Papers, part of the Texas Confederate Museum Collection archived at the Haley History Center, was limited to an examination of issues directly pertaining to the Palmito Battlefield site.[1] But certainly future research into local, state, federal (particularly Union field and after-action reports regarding the First Battle of Palmito Ranch), and even international records (such as Juan N. Cortina's Mexican military service records), could shed additional light on the events that occurred there in the waning moments of the most disastrous military conflict in US history.

There is ample evidence within the documents surveyed to strongly suggest that the Ford Papers hold much valuable information regarding a wide variety of issues. For example, there are numerous documents concerning the official administration of the Western Subdistrict of Texas during the Civil War (including the long-standing contentious relationship between Ford and General Slaughter); Ford's service as a Texas Ranger, politician, and ardent secessionist; and various other items of historical importance to Texas and the United States. One issue of particular note is the oft-disputed cross-border cotton trade. The Ford Papers contain substantial amounts of correspondence and official orders related to that matter, casting some doubt on the idea promulgated by many historians that such trade was minimal and insignificant. The fact is that blood was spilled, even though peace was in sight. Whatever a researcher's topic of interest, the detailed indexes created by Haley Library archivists Jim Bradshaw and Cathy Smith allow researchers to easily develop their own list of potentially relevant materials, some possibly containing groundbreaking or myth-busting facts.[2]

Following the lead of the THC, other organizations have either enhanced their past efforts or have taken up the cause for the preservation of Palmito Ranch Battlefield NHL, interpretation of the Civil War in South Texas, and promotion of heritage tourism of the site. For example Texas Tech University's Department of Landscape Architecture has made efforts to formulate a comprehensive preservation planning document for the Battle of Palmito Ranch; and the University of Texas Rio Grande Valley has established the Community Historical Archaeological Project with Schools (CHAPS) and the Rio Grande Valley Civil War Trail—a consortium of communities working to develop heritage tourism focused on the Civil War over a two hundred–mile portion of the lower Rio Grande.

The population is growing dramatically in the counties bordering the Rio Grande in deep South Texas. Issues relating to livability and education are of paramount importance, and it is fair to say that the role of the THC and the local and federal entities engaged in natural resource (e.g., birding) and heritage tourism will continue to play larger roles in the ongoing preservation and interpretation of the battlefield.

In time for the sesquicentennial of the Civil War, the THC continued its effort with the writing of this book and a new replica marker project for the battlefield. For the construction and operation of the SpaceX Texas Launch Site at the terminus of State Highway 4, in southeastern Cameron County, and within close proximity to the eastern boundary of Palmito Ranch Battlefield NHL, SpaceX agreed to a number of mitigation measures. The first consisted of the placement of a replica 1936 Texas Centennial Marker to replace the original, missing from the battlefield for nearly five decades. In March 2015, SpaceX funded the replication of the last marker for the Battle of Palmito Ranch in time for the battle's sesquicentennial in May. A month earlier, on April 11, the THC and its consortium of partners centered that year's Park Day around a discussion of the site's interpretation and the pending installation of the replica marker. This final Park Day before the sesquicentennial took its place within the tradition discussed throughout this book of presenting new interpretive activities to Park Day attendees to engage a larger audience in the battlefield's preservation. The marker's placement on May 19, 2015, one week after the sesquicentennial anniversary of the first day of the battle (postponed due to heavy rains during the anniversary date of May12–13), capped an impressive array of projects undertaken by the THC and its partners in preservation.[3]

Installation of the replica 1936 Texas Centennial Marker by Beall
Memorial next to the US Fish and Wildlife Service viewing platform,
Palmito Ranch Battlefield's core battlefield area, May 19, 2015
(courtesy of the Texas Historical Commission).

The THC is committed to the concept of heritage tourism and believes in its financial and preservation value to Texans. Working with local and national stakeholders at Palmito Ranch Battlefield NHL through multiple projects toward the common goal of the battlefield's preservation for future generations served as the driving force for a series of undertakings from 2007 to 2015. Through this battlefield's history and well-preserved landscape, Texas students and history lovers alike can learn that the Civil War was not a distant conflict having little impact on their lives in Texas but a very real struggle that eventually made its way into their own state.

During the war, the position of the Confederate army in South Texas was as much for economic security as military protection. In response to the effective Union blockade of the Confederacy's coastlines, Southerners routed cotton grown west of the Mississippi through Texas across the border to Mexico and then shipped it to European textile mills. Appreciation of the two battles at Palmito Ranch adds to our understanding of the Civil War. Understanding the international implications associated with South Texas and Brownsville during the war reveals that it is no coincidence that both battles occurred where they did. Furthermore, in a broad context, the last land battle of the Civil War on May 12–13, 1865, represents more than the final land action of the war. The battle is an important part of the complex story about how the war ended in the field, not at the conference table. The battle was followed nearly one month later by Union Maj. Gen. Gordon Granger's dramatic reading in Galveston on June 19, 1865, of General Order No. 3 announcing that all of the slaves in Texas were free. Annual commemoration of this event is known today as Juneteenth. Together with the Battle of Palmito Ranch, they represent the final two links in the Civil War's chain of events that began at Fort Sumter, South Carolina, in April 1861 and ended in Texas more than four years later.

Heritage tourism to historic landmarks and sites contributes not only to the Texas economy but also to ourselves and what we value. "Sense of place is an essential asset for historic preservation, and Texans are deeply attached to their communities and to the heritage of Texas."[4] Palmito Ranch Battlefield NHL is a nonrenewable cultural and natural resource. If not protected, if its history is not preserved, if interpretation of its significance is not made available to all Americans, it can be lost forever. Some 150 years after the two battles that occurred there, the character of the landscape remains unspoiled because of the efforts of a diverse group. Preservation of Palmito

Ranch Battlefield NHL is possible today only because of the hard work of the US Fish and Wildlife Service's South Texas Refuge Complex, the Civil War Trust, the National Park Service's Palo Alto Battlefield National Historical Park, the Brownsville Historical Association, the Rio Grande Valley Civil War Trail, several independent historians and archeologists, engaged local landowners, and the Cameron County Historical Commission. When married to the effort by the THC, the Friends of the Texas Historical Commission, and the generous financial support of several donors, the battlefield's preservation is more assured today than it has ever been, and the site can serve as an educational tool for years to come. Visiting this battlefield should be at the top of any Texas Civil War history enthusiast's list.[5]

Notes

INTRODUCTION

1. Carrington, "The Last Battle," 434.

2. "Texas in the Civil War," brochure, 2013, 3, Texas Historical Commission (THC), Military Sites Program, "Civil War Project" files.

3. Campbell, *Gone to Texas*, 287–90; Holcomb, "Tell It Like It Was," 181–96; Cantrell and Turner, *Lone Star Pasts*, 5–7.

4. "Texas in the Civil War," brochure.

5. Oates, *Rip Ford's Texas*.

6. Trudeau, *Out of the Storm*, 299–310.

7. Tucker, *The Final Fury*, 52.

8. Ibid., 158–60.

9. Hunt, *The Last Battle of the Civil War*, 169–71, 117–19, 127–28. See also US War Department, *War of the Rebellion*, 266–67.

10. Hunt, *The Last Battle of the Civil War*, 128.

11. Ibid., 11, 22, 23, 78, 89, 97, 100, 108, 177–98, 161–62. Ford's role in the two battles at Palmito Ranch, and his other actions related to those clashes, is more thoroughly recounted in McCaslin, *Fighting Stock*.

12. The Ford Papers were not available to Hunt at the time he was conducting his research for his book on the Battle of Palmito Ranch, as they were in the process of being catalogued and properly preserved at their new home in West Texas.

13. Terri Myers, "Palmito Ranch Battlefield National Historic Landmark" nomination, 1997, 31, THC, Military Sites Program.

14. Douglas Murphy and Nancy Brown, memo about upcoming viewing platform at the battlefield, November 2011, THC, Military Sites Program, "Civil War Project" files; Myers, "Palmito Ranch Battlefield National Historic Landmark" nomination, 10.

15. McWhorter, "Lone Star Leadership," 1; Myers, "Palmito Ranch Battlefield National Historic Landmark" nomination, 12–13.

16. Tucker, *The Final Fury*, ix; Hunt, *The Last Battle of the Civil War*, 70; US War Department, *War of the Rebellion*, 265.

17. Myers, "Palmito Ranch Battlefield National Historic Landmark" nomination, 1; Cameron County Historical Commission, *1990 Annual Report to the Texas Historical Commission*, December 10, 1990, 1–2; and Office of State Auditor and Efficiency Expert, *Report of an Examination of the Texas Centennial*, 1939, 91, both in THC.

18. Rutgers University and University of Texas at Austin, *Economic Impact of Historic Preservation in Texas*, an executive summary for the THC, 2015, 7, THC.

19. Ibid.

Chapter 1

1. "Texas in the Civil War," brochure, 2–4, THC, Military Sites Program, "Civil War Project" files; Haley, *Sam Houston*.

2. "Texas in the Civil War," brochure, 4; "Hispanics and the Civil War: From Battlefield to Homefront," 2012, National Park Service.

3. "Texas in the Civil War," brochure, 14; Campbell, "Slavery."

4. "Texas in the Civil War," brochure, 2. Also see Sands, *Reefer to Rear-Admiral*, 278; "Juneteenth" documents, 2014, "Marker Program" file, THC.

5. Campbell, *Gone to Texas*, 239–41.

6. Ibid., 241.

7. McCaslin, *Fighting Stock*, 101–11, 122.

8. Ibid., 107–12, 120.

9. Ibid., 113–20, 123–27.

10. Campbell, *Gone to Texas*; Harrison, *Alleyton*; Britton, Elliott, and Miller, "Cotton Culture"; and Becker and Hamilton, "Wartime Cotton Trade."

11. McCaslin, *Fighting Stock*, 120.

12. Ibid.

13. Ibid., 120–21.

Chapter 2

1. McCaslin, *Fighting Stock*, 120–21.

2. Ibid. There are many documents in the Ford Papers and elsewhere, cited by McCaslin, that indicate the high morale of the troops who remained with Ford in May 1865.

3. For example, see Ford Papers, TCM94.40.A1–2B1–3, 6.1, D6, 12, E1, 8, 10, G1–4.166; TCM94.1.0358, 0845, 1029, 1032, 1034, 0844.

4. Ibid., TCM94.40.A1–2B1–3, 6.1, D6, 12, E1, 8, 10, G1–4.166; TCM94.1.0358, 0486, 1029, 1032, 1034, 0844–5, 0541, 0547; TCM94.1.0073.

5. Ibid., TCM94.40.D6, E10; TCM94.1.0359–61; TCM94.1.0261.

6. Ibid., TCM94.40.1.D-5; TCM94.1.0845.

7. Ibid., TCM94.1.0844.

8. Ibid., TCM94.1.0846.

9. Ibid., TCM94.40.1.D6.

10. Ibid.

11. Ibid.; McCaslin, *Fighting Stock*, 117–18.

12. Ford Papers, TCM94.1.720–21; Thompson, *Cortina*, 140–45. The Rio Grande was officially recognized as the northern border of Mexico at the signing of the Treaty of Guadalupe Hildalgo in 1848; therefore, Cortina's involvement in the battle in September 1864 was an illegal interference in the internal dispute of a sovereign nation. See Kent, "Constitution and the Laws of War during the Civil War," 1856–60.

13. Ford Papers, TCM94.1.363.

14. Ibid.

15. Ibid.

16. Ibid.

17. Ibid., TCM94.1.0935; Robertson, *Wild Horse Desert*, 122–26.

18. Ford Papers, TCM94.40.1.F2, 7.5; TCM94.1.0362.

19. Ibid., TCM94.1.0361.

20. Ibid., TCM94.1.0360; TCM94.1.0362.

21. Ibid., TCM94.1.0359.

22. Ibid., TCM94.1.0541.a, b.

23. Ibid., TCM94.1.0540.

24. Ibid., TCM94.1.542.

25. Ibid., TCM94.1.543.

26. Ibid., TCM94.1.547; TCM94.1.0073, 0545.

27. Ibid., TCM94.1.0536, 0552; TCM94.1.556, 0936, 0027, 006, 1257.

28. Ibid., TCM94.1.0261, 0263, 1260; Hunt, *Last Battle of the Civil War*, xi–xiv, 58–59.

CHAPTER 3

1. Myers, "Palmito Ranch Battlefield National Historic Landmark" nomination, 18, THC, Military Sites Program; further details on the "informal truce" are found in Hunt, *The Last Battle of the Civil War*, 35–38.

2. "Palmito Ranch Battlefield" files, THC, Military Sites Program; Ford Papers, TCM94.1.363.

3. Hunt, *The Last Battle of the Civil War*, 63–65; Myers, "Palmito Ranch Battlefield National Historic Landmark" nomination, 23–24.

4. Myers, "Palmito Ranch Battlefield National Historic Landmark" nomination, 23–24.

5. National Park Service, American Battlefield Protection Program grant project, "The Last Battle: Telling the Story of Palmito Ranch Battlefield" file, 2009, THC, Military Sites Program.

6. The following sources were all scoured for the best possible account of battlefield casualties: THC and the Friends of the Texas Historical Commission, National Park Service, American Battlefield Protection Program grant, "Palmito Ranch Battlefield National Historic Landmark Technical Report with Archeological Survey Report: Grant Number, GA-2255–09–008"; US War Department, *War of the Rebellion*, 266–67. Palo Alto Battlefield National Historic Site historian Douglas Murphy, in a November 2011 memo for the US Fish and Wildlife Service, indicates that the Union records accounted for two killed, twenty-eight wounded, and more than one hundred captured. An article in the Brownsville *Herald* published on April 12, 1936, "Last Battle of Civil War Was Fought near Brownsville Long after Lee Had Surrendered, and When Both Armies Knew It!," reported that 115 Union soldiers (111 enlisted and 4 officers) and a handful of Confederates were killed in action. (The article is on microfilm on file at University of Texas–Pan American library.) The 1997 National Historic Landmark nomination for Palmito Ranch Battlefield states, "Historians still debate the number of casualties for each side. First hand reports report light casualties for both armies. Barrett reports 111 Federal casualties total, a number that includes both killed and wounded men, as well as those the Confederates captured. Rip Ford, in his handwritten memoirs, recalled that the Confederates only sustained seven casualties during the conflict; all seven men were wounded, he reported, and not killed." However, Stephen B. Oates, who produced the edited, organized version of Ford's memoir published in 1963, believes that about 30 Federal troops were killed and 113 more were taken prisoner, out of a total fighting force of 800. Oates theorized that the Confederates lost about the same number, although their total fighting force was much smaller, about 300 (*Rip Ford's Texas*, xxix). According to numerous accounts, Union troops died when they tried to swim across the Rio Grande in their panic to flee the conflict.

7. Ford Papers, TCM94.1.1247.

8. Hunt, *Last Battle of the Civil War*, 15; Ford Papers, TCM94.40.B1–6.1, D12, E1, 8, 10, G1–2.

9. Ford Papers, TCM94.1.214; Hunt, *Last Battle of the Civil War*, 98.

10. Ford Papers, TCM94.40.A3.2, F1.10, G2.

11. Hunt, *Last Battle of the Civil War*, 48–49, 63.

12. Misulia, *Columbus, Georgia, 1865*, 233–47. Misulia is a Florida-based attorney, historical reenactor, and historic reproduction firearms manufacturer. The Battle of Columbus, Georgia, in April 1865 is his sole historical research

pursuit. Originally from Georgia, Misulia has long advocated for "official" recognition of his claim that the Battle of Columbus was the last "true" battle of the Civil War. His book, therefore, is essentially a position paper specifically created with that aim in mind. In it, Misulia dismisses the Palmito Ranch engagement based on his own arbitrary determination of how many troops there must be for an engagement to be considered a "true" battle rather than merely a "skirmish." Not surprisingly, the carefully crafted standard Misulia created conveniently fit the Battle of Columbus, while it narrowly excluded all others. This disregards the fact that military commanders on both sides of the conflict at the time unequivocally regarded Palmito Ranch as a battle, as has every military history scholar who has addressed it since then.

13. Ford Papers, TCM94.1.0073.

CHAPTER 4

1. Myers, "Palmito Ranch Battlefield National Historic Landmark" nomination, 1997, 9–15, THC, Military Sites Program.

2. Ibid.

3. "Interpretive Files on Civil War Veteran Reunion Movements Associated with the Confederate Reunion Ground State Historic Site," THC, Military Sites Program.

4. Garza and Long, "Cameron County."

5. "Texas in World War II, Cameron County files," THC, Military Sites Program; Garza and Long, "Cameron County."

6. Acreage determined from 1997 NHL nomination and the 1999 core battlefield report; Vela, *Cultural Resource Research, Identification and Documentation: National Park Service Resource Reconnaissance Survey*, 2001, 10, THC, Military Sites Program.

7. Garza and Long, "Cameron County."

8. Lower Rio Grande Valley National Wildlife Refuge, US Fish and Wildlife Service, accessed April 29, 2014, http://www.fws.gov/refuge/Lower_Rio_Grande_Valley/.

9. Brinkman, "Gifts of Granite, Bequests of Bronze"; Office of State Auditor and Efficiency Expert, *Report of an Examination of the Texas Centennial*, Austin 1939, 85, THC. Weighing twenty-two hundred pounds, these centennial monuments were quarried in Llano County.

10. Commission of Control for Texas Centennial Celebrations, *Monuments Erected by the State of Texas*, 123, 151, 203; "Monuments Erected over County to Mark Early Historic Events," Brownsville *Herald*, July 19, 1936; Office of State Auditor and Efficiency Expert, *Report of an Examination of the Texas Centennial*, 85, 91.

11. Jones, *Texas Testimony Carved in Stone*, 50; Commission of Control for Texas Centennial Celebrations, *Monuments Erected by the State of Texas*, 151.

12. "Last Battle of Civil War Was Fought near Brownsville Long after Lee Had Surrendered, and When Both Armies Knew It!," Brownsville *Herald*, April 12, 1936. See also Texas State Library and Archives Commission, Box 2000/021–11, Correspondence re: county commissions, 1963–1964; Cameron County, 1962–1964; Folder Cameron County, 1962–1964; letter from the Cameron County Historical Survey Committee to the Texas State Historical Survey Committee, August 17, 1964; letter from the Cameron County Historical Survey Committee to the Texas State Historical Survey Committee, August 18, 1964.

13. US Congress, H.J. Res. 253, 85th Cong., joint resolution to establish a commission to commemorate the one hundredth anniversary of the Civil War, and for other purposes it became Public Law 85–305 on September 7, 1957; Texas State Library and Archives Commission, Texas State Historical Survey Committee file, Box 808–2, Confederate Memorial Information Markers Case files, 1962–65, Texas Civil War Centennial Advisory Committee (1963) folder; and letter from Governor Connally to the Texas State Historical Survey Committee, July 12, 1963.

14. Governor John Connally to John Ben Shepperd, president of the Texas State Historical Survey Committee, July 12, 1963, referencing transfer of the duties given to the Texas Civil War Centennial Commission to the Texas State Historical Survey Committee, Texas State Historical Survey Committee file, Box 808–2, Texas Civil War Centennial Advisory Committee folder, Texas State Library and Archives Commission, Austin.

15. Press release distributed by the Texas State Historical Survey Committee, December 17, 1963, Texas State Historical Survey Committee file, Box 808–3, Confederate Memorial Information Markers case files, 1962–1965, Brazos Santiago C.S.A. (1963) folder, Texas State Library and Archives Commission.

16. The Battle of Palmito Hill 1963 marker was one of many special Tourist Information Markers made that year, evidently as a joint project of the Texas State Historical Survey Committee (the THC today), the Texas Game and Fish Commission, the Texas Highway Department, and Texas State Parks Board. The Game and Fish Commission and Parks Board are now part of the Texas Parks and Wildlife Department. There were twenty-two such markers made, nineteen by Sewah Studios in Ohio (including the Battle of Palmito Hill) and three by the Southwell Company in San Antonio.

17. Letter from the Cameron County Historical Survey Committee to the Texas State Historical Survey Committee, January 28, 1964; letter from the Cameron County Historical Survey Committee to the Texas State Historical Survey Committee, August 18, 1964, in Correspondence re: County Commissions, 1963–1964, Box 2000/021/11, Folder Cameron County, 1962–1964, Texas State Library and Archives Commission.

18. Texas State Library and Archives Commission, Box 2000/021–7, Correspondence re: county commissions, 1963–1964, Cameron County, 1962–1964, Folder Cameron County, 1962–1964; letter from the Cameron County Historical Survey Committee to the Texas State Historical Survey Committee, August 17, 1964; letter from the Cameron County Historical Survey Committee to the Texas State Historical Survey Committee, February 8, 1965; Texas State Library and Archives Commission, Box 2000/021–7, Correspondence re: county commissions, 1963–1964, Cameron County, 1962–1964, Folder Cameron County, 1962–1964; letter from the Cameron County Historical Survey Committee to the Texas State Historical Survey Committee, August 17, 1964; letter from the Cameron County Historical Survey Committee to the Texas State Historical Survey Committee, August 18, 1964; THC Marker Program file for the Battle of Palmito Ranch, 1990; and letter from the Texas State Historical Survey Committee to the Cameron County Historical Survey Committee, October 2, 1968. Hurricane Beulah struck South Texas in September 1967.

19. THC, Marker Program file for the Battle of Palmito Ranch; Cameron County Historical Commission, *1990 Annual Report to the Texas Historical Commission*, December 10, 1990, 1–2, THC.

20. THC, Marker Program file for the Battle of Palmito Ranch.

21. Ibid. It is noteworthy that all three historic markers placed by the state of Texas (1936, 1964, and 1990) have lacked the "Lost Cause" interpretation that had often found its way into the historical narratives of Civil War sites, both inside and outside Texas.

22. David Moore, Terri Myers, Matt Goebel, and the National Register Program of the THC are responsible for this milestone in verifying the historic significance of the battlefield in the 1993 National Register of Historic Places nomination. Palmito Ranch Battlefield National Historic Landmark, 1997, 9, THC; and letter from the US Fish and Wildlife Service to the THC, July 7, 1994, THC, Military Sites Program.

23. Grear, *The Fate of Texas*, 182.

Chapter 5

1. Civil War Trust, accessed June 1, 2016, https://www.civilwar.org/.

2. The Civil War Trust purchased slightly more than three acres on November 28, 2001, for thirty thousand dollars. E-mail and phone correspondence between the THC and Tom Gilmore, director of real estate with the Civil War Trust, November 2007, THC, Military Sites Program.

3. Grear, *The Fate of Texas*, 183.

4. The South Texas Refuge Complex, US Fish and Wildlife Service, accessed June 1, 2016, https://www.fws.gov/southwest/refuges/texas/STRC/.

5. E-mail and phone correspondence between the THC and the US Fish and Wildlife Service, fall 2007, THC, Military Sites Program.

6. "Palmito Ranch Battlefield" files, THC, Military Sites Program.

7. Letter from David Vela, superintendent, Palo Alto Battlefield National Historic Site, to the THC, June 18, 2001, "Palmito Ranch Battlefield" files, THC, Military Sites Program. The Vela letter accompanied a copy of the National Park Service's *National Park Service Resource Reconnaissance Survey* (2001), 7, 8.

8. Letter from [Leann Biles] of the THC to US senator Kay Bailey Hutchison, November 1, 2001, "Palmito Ranch Battlefield" files, THC, Military Sites Program.

9. "Palmito Ranch Battlefield" files, THC, Military Sites Program.

10. On April 5, 2008, the THC and the Jefferson County Historical Commission co-hosted Park Day at Sabine Pass Battleground. William A. McWhorter was joined by THC staff—Efrem Hill, Kristie Lawler, and Deputy Director Terry Colley.

11. McWhorter, "Lone Star Leadership."

12. Ibid.

13. "Sabine Pass Battleground State Historic Site" files, THC, Military Sites Program.

14. Douglas Murphy informed the THC of the existence of the report on the project undertaken when David Vela was superintendent of Palo Alto Battlefield National Historic Site. See *Battlefield Core Area Identification Report*, Palo Alto Battlefield National Historic Site, National Park Service, in THC, Military Sites Program.

15. E-mail and phone correspondence between the THC and Palo Alto Battlefield National Historic Site, 2008, "Palmito Ranch Battlefield" files, THC, Military Sites Program.

16. E-mail and phone correspondence between the THC and the US Fish and Wildlife Service, Cameron County Historical Commission, and the National Park Service, 2008, "Palmito Ranch Battlefield" files, THC, Military Sites Program.

17. This grant turned out to be the first of four grants for the Military Sites Program from the SOSC between 2008 and 2011 that enhanced the historical record of the battlefield and helped provide interpretive mediums for the battlefield. Friends of the Texas Historical Commission contract with Jody Edward Ginn, 2008, THC, Military Sites Program.

18. Fortuitously for Military Sites Program Coordinator William McWhorter, within the THC he had the support of his immediate supervisor, History Programs Division Director Bratten Thomason, and others. Director of the Friends of the Texas Historical Commission at this time was the talented and experienced Toni Turner. Turner coordinated the Military Sites Program's 2008 grant application with the SOSC. An accomplished historian and author, Turner and her husband, James Bruseth, then division director for the THC's Archeological

Division, had previously coauthored the award-winning book *From a Watery Grave*. Upon consultation with McWhorter, Turner recruited Bruseth to help develop a grant application in early 2009 that would require all of their talents—an archeological survey atop Palmito Hill.

19. E-mail from Katherine Faz to William McWhorter, May 31, 2009, "Palmito Ranch Battlefield" files, THC, Military Sites Program.

20. In April 2009, the US Congress passed legislation that expanded Palo Alto Battlefield National Historic Site to include Resaca de la Palma (another Mexican-American War battlefield), and the national park's name changed to Palo Alto Battlefield National Historical Park.

21. E-mail and phone correspondence between the THC and the National Park Service, "Palmito Ranch Battlefield" files, THC, Military Sites Program.

22. Palo Alto Battlefield staff present that day included Superintendent Mary Kralovec, Historian Douglas Murphy, and Archeologist/Resource Management Chief Rolando Garza.

23. Through its chairpersons Larry Lof, Mary Torres, Betty Agado, Wilson Bourgeois, and Steve Hathcock, the Cameron County Historical Commission has taken an active and ever-increasing role in the preservation of the Palmito Ranch Battlefield since 2007.

Chapter 6

1. *Battlefield Core Area Identification Report*, Palo Alto National Battlefield National Historic Site, National Park Service; and Vela, *Cultural Resource Research, Identification and Documentation*, both on file at the THC, Military Sites Program.

2. THC and the Friends of the Texas Historical Commission, National Park Service, American Battlefield Protection Program grant, "Palmito Ranch Battlefield National Historic Landmark Technical Report with Archeological Survey Report: Grant Number, GA-2255–09–008," 2009. The ABPP also funded the 2001 Cultural Resource Research, Identification and Documentation National Park Service Resource Reconnaissance Survey.

3. Haecker, Garza, and Morris, *An Historical Archeological Perspective of the Battlefield of Palmito Ranch*, 12.

4. Ibid., 50.

5. Ibid., 29.

6. US War Department, *War of the Rebellion*, 266, 268.

7. Jody E. Ginn, *Palmito Ranch Battlefield Site: Report from the Papers of Colonel John Salmon (Rip) Ford*, 2010, Nita Stewart Haley Memorial Library and J. Evetts Haley History Center, Midland, Texas, and THC, Military Sites Program.

8. Hunt, *Last Battle of the Civil War*, 70–71.

9. US War Department, *War of the Rebellion*, 266, 268.

10. Myers, "Palmito Ranch Battlefield National Historic Landmark" nomination, 1997, 23, THC, Military Sites Program.

11. US War Department, *War of the Rebellion*, 266.

12. Archeological projects conducted by the THC (the State Historic Preservation Office for the State of Texas) meet, follow, and whenever possible exceed the secretary of the interior's "Standards and Guidelines for Archeology and Historic Preservation" and Section 110 of the National Historic Preservation Act.

13. Vela, *Cultural Resource Research, Identification and Documentation*.

CHAPTER 7

1. US Fish and Wildlife Service memo via e-mail from Bryan Winton, Santa Ana National Wildlife Refuge manager, to William A. McWhorter, December 21, 2009, THC, Military Sites Program. As part of this initiative, a third sign was placed at the South Texas Refuge Complex near Alamo to help direct birding and natural resource tourists to Palmito Ranch Battlefield NHL.

2. THC and the Friends of the Texas Historical Commission, Challenge Cost Share grant with the US Fish and Wildlife Services (FWS Agreement Number 20181-A-J626), "Exploring the Boundaries: Palmito Ranch Battlefield National Historic Landmark, TX," for the radio broadcast repeater system and signage project, THC, Military Sites Program.

3. Friends of the Texas Historical Commission, application to the Society of the Order of the Southern Cross, 2010, on file at the Friends of the Texas Historical Commission.

CHAPTER 8

1. During the 80th Legislative Session, House Bill 12 transferred eighteen historic properties from the Texas Parks and Wildlife Department to the THC. The same bill authorized the THC to operate the historic sites under the Texas Parks and Wildlife Code until such time that the state code could be amended. Senate Bill 1518 amends the code to provide the THC with the authority to operate the sites and establish any and all procedures for operating the sites. See Texas State Legislature, "Analysis of Bill" and "Fiscal Note."

2. Communication with the Civil War Trust, regarding possible donation of three acres of Palmito Hill, Cameron County, Texas, THC, Military Sites Program.

3. Military Sites Program's Short-Form Program Proposal regarding accepting three acres of Palmito Ranch Battlefield, October 2012, THC, Military Sites Program.

4. "Palmito Ranch Battlefield" files, THC, Military Sites Program.

5. Ibid.

6. "Palmito Ranch Battlefield" files, THC, Military Sites Program.

7. Rutgers University and the University of Texas at Austin, *Economic Impact of Historic Preservation in Texas*, an executive summary for the THC, 2015, 12–13. For this study, a heritage traveler is one who cited "visit a historic site" as a primary activity. These travelers spent roughly $7.3 billion in trip expenditures in 2013. It would, however, be unfair to credit the full $7.3 billion to heritage tourism—this figure includes, for example, all the spending of a Texas business traveler to San Antonio who also visited the Alamo. To calculate the specific economic impact of heritage-related activities, the share of overall travel expenditures focused directly on heritage activity was estimated. This yielded a heritage-attributed outlay estimate of nearly $2.3 billion in 2013. This total was then used to estimate the full economic impact of heritage travel spending.

8. Rio Grande Valley Civil War Trail, University of Texas Rio Grande, accessed August 1, 2017, www.utrgv.edu/civilwar-trail.

9. Cameron County Historical Commission, Civil War Sesquicentennial Committee, PH150 brochure, THC, Military Sites Program.

10. Ibid.

Epilogue

1. "Palmito Ranch Battlefield" files, THC, Military Sites Program.

2. "Last Battle of Civil War Was Fought near Brownsville after Lee Surrendered, and When Both Armies Knew It!," Brownsville *Herald*, April 12, 1936. Microfilm on file at library, University of Texas–Pan American.

3. "Palmito Ranch Battlefield" files, THC, Military Sites Program.

4. Rutgers University and University of Texas at Austin, *Economic Impact of Historic Preservation in Texas*, an executive summary for the THC, updated 2015, 56, THC.

5. Partial notes are from Leann Biles's report of the Civil War Preservation Trust Discovery Trail, THC, Military Sites Program; Rutgers University and the University of Texas at Austin, *Economic Impact of Historic Preservation in Texas*, 54.

Bibliography

Archives

Cameron County Historical Commission, Brownsville, Texas
Box 2000/02177, Correspondence
Ford, John S. Papers. The Nita Stewart Haley Memorial Library and J. Evetts Haley
    History Center, Texas Confederate Museum Collection, Midland, Texas
Friends of the Texas Historical Commission, Austin, Texas
Texas Historical Commission, Austin, Texas
Battle of Palmito Ranch files
Civil War Project files
Historical Marker file
Marker Program file
Military Sites Program
Palmito Ranch Battlefield files
Sabine Pass Battleground State Historic Site files
Texas in World War II, Cameron County files
Texas State Historical Survey Committee files
Box 808–2, Confederate Memorial Information Markers case files
Box 808–3, Confederate Memorial Information Markers case files
Box 2000/021–7, Correspondence
Box 2000/21–11, Correspondence

Secondary Sources

Barrett, Col. Theodore H. *Report to Headquarters, First Division, 25th Army
    Corps: August 10, 1865.* In US War Department, *War of the Rebellion: A
    Compilation of the Official Records of the Union and Confederate Armies,* Se-
    ries 1, vol. 48, pt. 1. Washington, DC: US Government Printing Office, 1896.
Becker, Jack, and Matthew K. Hamilton. "Wartime Cotton Trade." In *Hand-*

book of Texas Online. Accessed May 15, 2015. http://www.tshaonline.org/handbook/online/articles/drw01. Uploaded on June 28, 2012. Modified on September 4, 2013. Published by the Texas State Historical Association.

Branson, Lt. Col. David. *Report to Headquarters, Sixty-Second Regiment US Colored Infantry: May 18, 1865*. In US War Department, *War of the Rebellion: A Compilation of the Official Records of the Union and Confederate Armies*, Series 1, vol. 48, pt. 1. Washington, DC: US Government Printing Office, 1896.

Brinkman, Bob. "Gifts of Granite, Bequests of Bronze." *Historical Markers Program Coordinator* (blog), Texas Historical Commission, May 13, 2014. http://www.thc.texas.gov/blog/gifts-granite-bequests-bronze.

Britton, Karen Gerhardt, Fred C. Elliott, and E. A. Miller. "Cotton Culture." In *Handbook of Texas Online*. Accessed May 15, 2015. https://tshaonline.org/handbook/online/articles/afc03. Uploaded on June 12, 2012. Published by the Texas State Historical Association.

Bruseth, James E., and William T. Pierson. "Large-Area Remote Sensing Coverage of Archaeological Sites with a Dual-Track Cart-Mounted Cesium Magnetometer." *Journal of Field Archaeology* 32 (2007): 133–48.

Campbell, Randolph B. *Gone to Texas: A History of the Lone Star State*. 2nd ed. New York: Oxford University Press, 2012.

———. "Slavery." In *Handbook of Texas Online*. Accessed November 2, 2016. http://www.tshaonline.org/handbook/online/articles/yps01. Uploaded on June 15, 2010. Modified on July 26, 2017. Published by the Texas State Historical Association.

Cantrell, Gregg, and Elizabeth Hayes Turner, eds. *Lone Star Pasts: Memory and History in Texas*. College Station: Texas A&M University Press, 2007.

Carrington, W. H. D. "The Last Battle—the Last Charge, and the Last Gun Fired in the War." In *History of Texas*, vol. 2, *From 1685 to 1892*, by John Henry Brown, 431–43. 1892. Reprint, Austin: Jenkins Publishing, 1970.

Civil War Sites Advisory Commission. *Report on the Nation's Civil War Battlefields*. Washington, DC: National Park Service, 1993. https://www.nps.gov/abpp/cwsac/cws0–1.html.

Commission of Control for Texas Centennial Celebrations. *Monuments Erected by the State of Texas to Commemorate the Centenary of Texas Independence*. Austin: Steck, 1939.

Garza, Alicia A., and Christopher Long. 2012. "Cameron County." In *Handbook of Texas Online*. Accessed May 25, 2012. http://tshaonline.org/handbook/online/articles/hcc04. Uploaded on June 12, 2012. Modified on August 31, 2016. Published by the Texas State Historical Association.

Grear, Charles D., ed. *The Fate of Texas: The Civil War and the Lone Star State*. Fayetteville: University of Arkansas Press, 2008.

Haecker, Charles M., Rolando Garza, and Charles Morris. *An Historical Archeological Perspective of the Battle of Palmito Ranch*, *"The Last Conflict of the*

Great Rebellion." Washington, DC: National Park Service, Heritage Partnership Programs, 2003.

Haley, James L. *Sam Houston.* Norman: University of Oklahoma Press, 2002.

Harrison, William H. *Alleyton: Texas Back Door to the Confederacy.* Columbus, TX: Show-Me Type & Print, 1993.

Holcomb, Julie. "Tell It Like It Was." In *The Fate of Texas: The Civil War and the Lone Star State*, ed. Charles D. Grear, 181–96. Fayetteville: University of Arkansas Press, 2008.

Hunt, Jeffrey William. *The Last Battle of the Civil War: Palmetto Ranch.* Austin: University of Texas Press, 2002.

Jones, William M. *Texas Testimony Carved in Stone.* Houston: Scardino Printing, 1952.

Kent, Andrew. "Constitution and the Laws of War during the Civil War: The Federal Courts, Practice and Procedure." *Notre Dame Law Review* 85, no. 5 (2009–10): 1839, 1856–60.

Manning, Dan R. *John James Dix: A Texian.* Springfield, MO: Goldminds Publishing, 2008.

McCaslin, Richard B. *Fighting Stock: John S. Rip Ford in Texas.* Fort Worth: TCU Press, 2011.

McWhorter, William. "Lone Star Leadership: Preserving the Hallowed Ground of Texas at Palmito Ranch and Sabine Pass." *Hallowed Ground* 10, no. 4 (2009): 18–25. https://www.civilwar.org/learn/articles/lone-star-leadership.

Misulia, Charles A. *Columbus, Georgia, 1865: The Last True Battle of the Civil War.* Tuscaloosa: University of Alabama Press, 2010.

"Monuments Erected over County to Mark Early Historic Events." *Brownsville Herald*, July 19, 1936. https://www.newspapers.com/newspage/23790351/.

Oates, Stephen B., ed. *Rip Ford's Texas: By John Salmon Ford.* Austin: University of Texas Press, 1963.

Robertson, Brian. *Wild Horse Desert: The Heritage of South Texas.* Edinburg, TX: New Santander Press, 1985.

Sands, Benjamin F. *Reefer to Rear-Admiral: Reminiscences and Journal Jottings of Nearly Half a Century of Naval Life.* New York: Frederick A. Stokes, 1899.

Scott, Douglas, Lawrence Babits, and Charles M. Haecker. *Fields of Conflict: Battlefield Archaeology from the Roman Empire to the Korean War.* Dulles, VA: Potomac Books, 2007.

Texas State Legislature. "Analysis of Bill." 80th Legislative Session, May 17, 2007. http://www.legis.state.tx.us/tlodocs/80R/analysis/html/HB00012E.htm.

———. "Fiscal Note, 82nd Legislative Regular Session." May 3, 2011. http://www.legis.state.tx.us/Search/DocViewer.aspx?ID=82RSB015183F&QueryText=%22SB1518%22&DocType=F.

Thompson, Jerry. *Cortina: Defending the Mexican Name in Texas.* College Station: Texas A&M University Press, 2007.

Trudeau, Noah Andre. *Out of the Storm: The End of the Civil War, April–June 1865.* New York: Little, Brown, 1994.

Tucker, Philip Thomas. *The Final Fury: Palmito Ranch, the Last Battle of the Civil War.* Mechanicsburg, PA: Stackpole, 2001.

US War Department. *War of the Rebellion: A Compilation of the Official Records of the Union and Confederate Armies.* Series 1, vol. 48, pt. 1. Washington, DC: US Government Printing Office, 1896.

Index